MODEL ANIMAL WELFARE ACT

– A Comprehensive Framework Law –

Janice H. Cox, MBA

Dr. iur. Sabine Lennkh

World Animal Net

Design by Jessica Bridgers

Copyediting by Amy J. Chin

This print version of the
MODEL ANIMAL WELFARE ACT
was made possible by donations from:

International Fund for Animal Welfare
World Wide Animal Rescue
Pegasus Foundation
Pettus Crowe Foundation

With special thanks to:

Wim de Kok

for his support in making this book a reality

Connecting the Animal Protection Movement

World Animal Net
25 Chestnut Square
Boston, MA 02130
USA

www.worldanimal.net
info@worldanimal.net

For more about the Model Animal
Welfare Act visit ModelAWA.org

© 2016 World Animal Net

All rights reserved. Reproduction or modification
for distribution or republication is permitted only
with prior written consent of World Animal Net.

Printed in the United States of America

First printing, 2016

ISBN 978-0-692-80315-8

ACKNOWLEDGEMENTS

World Animal Net would like to thank the following individuals and organisations for kindly reviewing the Model Animal Welfare Act, and providing valuable comments and suggestions for its improvement. We greatly appreciate the generous sharing of your considerable expertise and experience in this field.

Akisha Townsend Eaton, Esq., Senior Policy and Legal Resource Advisor, World Animal Net.

Amanda S. Whitfort BA (Hons)/LLB (Monash)/LLM (London), Associate Professor, Faculty of Law, The University of Hong Kong.

Dr. Antoine Goetschel, President of the GAL Project; & Sabine Brels, Manager of the GAL Project.

Carney Anne Nasser, Esq., Legislative Counsel, Animal Legal Defense Fund.

David Favre, J.D., Professor of Animal Law, Michigan State University, Editor-in-Chief of Animal Legal & Historical Web Center.

Emmanuel Giuffre, Legal Counsel of Voiceless, the animal protection institute (Australia).

Jordi Casamitjana, Campaigns and Enforcement Manager of IFAW UK, BSc (Hons) Zoology.

Dr. Nick Palmer, Director of Policy, Cruelty Free International.

Drs. Noor Evertsen, Editor of the annual 'Teksten Wetgeving Dierenwelzijn' (Dutch animal welfare laws with an introduction) and Researcher and Consultant in Animal Law at Dier & Recht (Law & Justice for Animals).

Peter Stevenson, Chief Policy Advisor, Compassion in World Farming, Solicitor.

Ricardo Fajardo, Head of Policy and Advocacy at World Animal Protection, Colombian solicitor and author of the book El Derecho de los Animales ("Animal Law"), 2007.

Roly Owers, MRCVS, Chief Executive, World Horse Welfare.

Sarah Murphy, Consultant to World Animal Protection, Solicitor.

Web/Print Designer: Jessica Bridgers, M.S., Executive Director, World Animal Net.

Copy Editor: Amy J. Chin, World Animal Net.

AUTHORS/ RESEARCHERS

Dr. iur. Sabine Lennkh

Sabine Lennkh studied Law at the Ludwig-Maximilians-University in Munich, Germany. She is a fully qualified lawyer and completed her Doctorate at the University of Salzburg, Austria, specialising in Comparative Law and Animal Welfare Legislation. Her thesis was titled 'The Adaptation of European and Non-European Animal Welfare Law Models to the Seychelles' and in an extended version subsequently also published as a book. For over 10 years Dr. Lennkh has been exclusively active in the field of animal welfare legislation and has attended a number of international conferences and workshops in this context. She comments on draft animal welfare laws and writes legal articles on the subject. The focus of her research is in the sphere of legal comparison within international animal welfare laws and the drafting of animal welfare legislation. While acting as Deputy Chair for the Seychelles Society for the Prevention of Cruelty to Animals she was able to learn about the challenges of applied animal protection. Currently Sabine Lennkh is a Legislative Advisor for World Animal Net (WAN).

Janice H. Cox, MBA

Janice Cox has been working in animal protection for over 25 years, since leaving a UK government career to concentrate on achieving the social change needed to improve the lives of animals. During this time she held a number of Director-level positions in international animal protection organisations; including European Director and International Legislative Advisor to the World Society for the Protection of Animals (now World Animal Protection); International Development Director for Compassion in World Farming; and Co-Founder and Director/Trustee of World Animal Net. Janice Cox has worked extensively on animal welfare policy and legislation, including involvement in Council of Europe animal welfare working groups, the European Union (Executive Committee Member of the Eurogroup for Animals and EU lobbyist on animal experimentation issues); working as a consultant for the World Organisation for Animal Health (OIE)'s Southern African Representation on the development of their Regional Animal Welfare Strategy; and Consultant for the Pan African Animal Welfare Alliance (including researching and drafting regional animal welfare strategies/action plans). In addition to legislative and policy work, Janice Cox has managed practical animal welfare programmes around the world, and so also brings practical experience of animal welfare issues to the project.

MODEL ANIMAL WELFARE ACT

A Model Animal Welfare Act – Guiding Principles for Modern Animal Welfare Legislation, Proposal for the Wording of a New Animal Welfare Act, and Explanatory Notes

This Model Animal Welfare Act has been designed to serve as a basic template and guidance document for those interested in enacting new legislation or improving existing animal protection legislation. It has been drafted using an extensive comparative law exercise, taking into account 'best practice' in the field. Thus it is aspirational in nature; seeking to provide the best possible structures, systems and provisions to protect the welfare of animals. This may mean that countries which are just starting to establish animal welfare requirements might decide to introduce its provisions progressively. In such cases, a strategic approach (step-wise and prioritised) is recommended. This could also be considered in cases where countries already have structures, systems and provisions that have been introduced gradually over time, but remain less than optimal. The important principle is that each country works progressively towards the best possible protection for the welfare of its animal population, and indeed – as elaborated in the Three Rs approach – the eventual reduction and replacement of any uses of animals which compromise their welfare.

The purpose of this Model Animal Welfare Act is to function as an 'umbrella' or 'framework' law. Where a country has a federal system, it is recommended that it is introduced at national level (in preference to state, province or other regional levels). It represents an international unification and harmonisation of animal protection and welfare legislation, which can be adapted or modified – if the circumstances require – in Common Law as well as Civil Law systems. Elements of both legal orders have been considered and incorporated to achieve (as far as possible for the present day) a comprehensive, far-reaching and progressive approach to animal welfare legislation which takes account of the desired expedience when it comes to prevention of animal cruelty and abuse, establishing responsibility and the principle of care towards the animal, promoting the education and sensitisation of the population, as well as offering effective solutions for efficient law enforcement. This Model Act was created in order to govern people's behaviour, while other civil or religious legal systems may take a very different form (for example, be limited to 'codes' or 'edicts'). Nonetheless, elements of this Act can also be used for inspiration in creating, amending or interpreting these.

CONTENTS
IN BRIEF

CONTENTS

CONTENTS

CONTENTS

PART 1

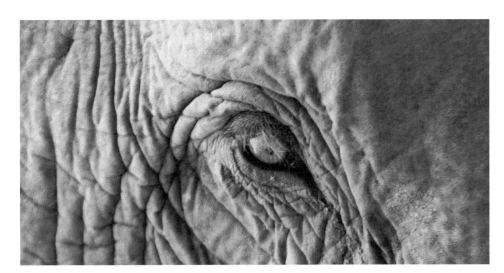

GUIDING PRINCIPLES FOR MODERN ANIMAL WELFARE LEGISLATION
– A BROAD OVERVIEW –

I. INTRODUCTION

Developments in Animal Welfare and Science

Animal welfare is increasingly acknowledged as an issue of major ethical and practical importance. Science has now confirmed that the sentient non-human animals who share our planet (and sometimes our lives) also share with us consciousness, emotions, feelings, perceptions – and the ability to experience pain, suffering and states of well-being. They are not 'objects' or 'things', and have not been considered as such in this Model Animal Welfare Act (Model AWA). Just like us they have biologically-determined natures, instincts and needs which are important to them. This underlines the necessity to acknowledge each individual animal's intrinsic value, and the fact that every single animal is not only worthy of respect and care, but also deserves to live a life that is meaningful without unnecessary human exploitation or interference.

Greater scientific knowledge and awareness have increased understanding of the importance of animal welfare; and this in turn has moved it from a marginal local or national concern to become an important regional and international policy issue. Animal welfare is now not only debated in regional and international policy forums, but is also covered by a fast-growing body of internationally and regionally accepted science-based policies, standards, conventions, treaties, regulations, directives and agreements.

Developments in Animal Welfare and International Policy

Today the World Organisation for Animal Health (still keeping its historical acronym of OIE: 'Office International des Épizooties') is the global standard setting body for animal welfare. At the request of its Member Countries, the OIE has been mandated to take the lead internationally on animal welfare and, as the international reference organisation for animal health, to elaborate recommendations and guidelines covering animal welfare. Animal Welfare was first identified as a priority for the OIE in the OIE Strategic Plan 2001 – 2005. Since May 2005, the World Assembly of OIE Delegates (representing each OIE Member Country and Territory) has adopted a body of international animal welfare standards, which are published in its Terrestrial Code and Aquatic Animal Health Standards Code (Aquatic Code). These standards are regularly updated to take account of latest scientific findings. The OIE continues to develop standards and recommendations in new areas of importance to animal welfare. These standards have been agreed by, and should be implemented by, each OIE Member Country. The OIE is also spearheading the formulation of Regional Animal Welfare Strategies (RAWS) for the progressive development of animal welfare across the various geographical regions, and these can include the introduction/improvement of legislation.

> Science has now confirmed that the sentient non-human animals who share our planet (and sometimes our lives) also share with us consciousness, emotions, feelings, perceptions – and the ability to experience pain, suffering and states of well-being.

The Food and Agricultural Organisation of the United Nations (FAO) is also active in the field of animal welfare, having established a portal called the 'Gateway to Animal Welfare' on its Web Site, which contains a wide range of information on animal welfare subjects. It also conducts thematic discussions and expert consultations, and has worked on animal welfare legislation.

In terms of Regional Economic Communities (RECs), the European Union (EU) is the most progressive one in regard to including animal welfare in its sphere of policy work. Its activities in this area are based on the recognition that animals are sentient beings. An amendment to the constitutional basis of the EU, the Treaty of Lisbon, which came into effect on 1st December 2009, now includes this principle and made it a binding condition to 'pay full regard to the welfare requirements of animals' when 'formulating and implementing' policies in relevant areas (which are specified). This puts animal welfare on an equal footing with other key principles such as: gender equality, social protection, human health, combat of discrimination, sustainable development, consumer protection and data protection. The EU has developed an extensive body of animal welfare legislation which has improved animal welfare standards across the REC, and helped to harmonise standards within its 'internal market' (thus reducing competitive distortions). It is formulating a new EU Strategy for the 'Protection and Welfare of Animals', which will include the consolidation of its animal welfare framework, more action to support compliance (particularly in terms of enforcement; implementation systems; the development of best practice and expertise; and education and awareness) and international cooperation.

"
The EU has also contributed significantly to raising the profile and awareness of animal welfare at an international level.

The EU has also contributed significantly to raising the profile and awareness of animal welfare at an international level – including through its collaboration with intergovernmental organisations such as the OIE and FAO; training and capacity building activities; and bilateral contacts (for example, including animal welfare in trade agreements with third countries).

Furthermore, these developments are not restricted to the 'Global North'. For instance, policy commitments to animal welfare are now also being developed across Africa – by important bodies such as the African Union (AU-IBAR) and some African Regional Economic Communities, as well as individual countries.

The Need for This Model Animal Welfare Act

These ethical, scientific and policy developments have led to many countries seeking to introduce or improve national animal welfare legislation. This Model Animal Welfare Act has been prepared to assist with this process. It has been formulated using a comparative analysis of the best available legislative models, precedents and advice; taking into account international standards and rules, and current knowledge based on animal welfare science and practical experience. It has also undergone an extensive consultation and evaluation procedure by international experts and institutions, which raised a multitude of helpful concerns and suggestions, all of which have contributed to the development of a deeply considered and more rounded proposal.

The most advanced modern animal welfare laws go beyond the traditional 'animal protection' or 'prevention of cruelty' statutes (which focus on protecting animals against human cruelty, i.e. deal with preventing acts of commission, as opposed to also including acts of omission). They are, in principal, now designed to meet the following three main requirements: to promote animal welfare, to prevent animal cruelty and to minimise the suffering of animals.

Furthermore, contemporary animal welfare legislation combines three core obligations. These are addressed to

The population – The duty of care (thus fostering the keeper's and handler's sense of responsibility towards the animal and ensuring that hence not only commission but also omission is covered by the law);

The state – The duty to create awareness, to inform, to educate and to support all issues of animal welfare; and

The authorities – The duty to effectively enforce the laws.

Defining Animal Welfare

The concept of animal welfare is evolving over time in line with ethical, scientific and policy developments. It is now more complex and developed than in early days when it was considered only in relation to absence of cruelty or 'unnecessary suffering'. Meanwhile it is generally defined using a number of concepts including: sentience; needs, interests and emotions; physical, mental and natural states ('telos'); and the five freedoms. This Model Animal Welfare Act takes account of these contemporary concepts of animal welfare, and is predicated on the belief that animals should have a good quality of life (enjoying physical, mental and emotional well-being; including the ability to live meaningful and natural lives, where they are able to meet their species-specific and ethological needs and behaviours) and a humane death.

> The concept of animal welfare is evolving over time in line with ethical, scientific and policy developments.

The definition of animal welfare currently used by the OIE is:

"Animal welfare means how an animal is coping with the conditions in which it lives. An animal is in a good state of welfare if (as indicated by scientific evidence) it is healthy, comfortable, well nourished, safe, able to express innate behaviour, and if it is not suffering from unpleasant states such as pain, fear, and distress."

"Good animal welfare requires disease prevention and appropriate veterinary treatment, shelter, management and nutrition, humane handling and humane slaughter or killing. Animal welfare refers to the state of the animal; the treatment that an animal receives is covered by other terms such as animal care, animal husbandry, and humane treatment."

The OIE has 'Guiding Principles for Animal Welfare', which were included in its Terrestrial Animal Health Code from 2004. These categorically state that: 'The use of animals carries with it an ethical responsibility to ensure the welfare of such animals to the greatest extent practicable.'

The Five Freedoms

Also included amongst the OIE's Guiding Principles are the internationally recognised 'Five Freedoms' which were originally published by the UK's Farm Animal Welfare Council (FAWC) in 1979 (although they originated in the 'Brambell Report', which dated back to 1965), and have been adapted slightly since their formulation. These are as follows:

1. **Freedom from Hunger and Thirst and Malnutrition** – by ready access to fresh water and a diet to maintain full health and vigour;
2. **Freedom from Fear and Distress** – by ensuring conditions and treatment which avoid mental suffering;
3. **Freedom from Physical and Thermal Discomfort** – by providing a suitable environment including shelter

and a comfortable resting area;

4. **Freedom from Pain, Injury and Disease** – by prevention or rapid diagnosis and treatment; and
5. **Freedom to Express Normal Patterns of Behaviour** – by providing sufficient space, proper facilities and company of the animal's own kind.

The 'Five Freedoms' provide valuable guidance on animal welfare needs; and they cover all three of the states identified above (physical, mental and natural states).

As a complement to the Five Freedoms, 12 criteria for the assessment of animal welfare have been identified by the Welfare Quality Project (WQP), a research partnership of scientists from Europe and Latin America funded by the European Commission. The WQP aims to develop a standardised system for assessing animal welfare – a system that would be implemented in Europe – and more generally to develop practical strategies and measures to improve animal welfare (Welfare Quality, 2009).

The 12 WQP criteria for the assessment of animal welfare are

1. Animals should not suffer from prolonged hunger, i.e. they should have a sufficient and appropriate diet.
2. Animals should not suffer from prolonged thirst, i.e. they should have a sufficient and accessible water supply.
3. Animals should have comfort around resting.
4. Animals should have thermal comfort, i.e. they should neither be too hot nor too cold.
5. Animals should have enough space to be able to move around freely.
6. Animals should be free of physical injuries.
7. Animals should be free of disease, i.e. farmers should maintain high standards of hygiene and care.
8. Animals should not suffer pain induced by inappropriate management, handling, slaughter or surgical procedures (e.g. castration, dehorning).
9. Animals should be able to express normal, non-harmful, social behaviours (e.g. grooming).
10. Animals should be able to express other normal behaviours, i.e. they should be able to express species-specific natural behaviours such as foraging.
11. Animals should be handled well in all situations, i.e. handlers should promote good human-animal relationships.
12. Negative emotions such as fear, distress, frustration or apathy should be avoided, whereas positive emotions such as security or contentment should be promoted.

The WQP criteria offer a useful framework for the development of legislation in line with international animal welfare principles. They have built on the Five Freedoms, developing more concrete and specific guidelines which may be more easily measured in practice (and particularly useful for legislative enforcement).

The 3Rs

The OIE's Guiding Principles for Animal Welfare also include the internationally recognised 'Three Rs' (3Rs) which provide valuable guidance for the use of animals in science. These are as follows:

1. Replacement of animals with non-animal techniques,
2. Reduction in numbers of animals, and
3. Refinement of experimental methods.

However, these should, in principle, additionally be applied to all commercial uses of animals where there is any doubt that all the welfare needs of the animals can be met, in which case the wording would need to be amended appropriately.

Together these important principles contain the fundamental precepts of animal welfare and protection, and currently form the foundations of various animal welfare policies, including those of the European Union.

One of the 'General Principles' of the 2008 Policy of the World Society for the Protection of Animals (WSPA), now World Animal Protection, was: "WSPA believes that where the welfare of an animal under human control is in question, then the animal must be given the benefit of any doubt. Furthermore, the different purposes for which animals are used must be regularly re-evaluated." This clearly promoted the 'precautionary principle' as regards any animal use. Furthermore, the Policy stated that "... where the needs of a species cannot be met, the species must not be kept by humans."

Creation and Modification of Animal Protection Legislation

As regards primary legislation, a national framework Act is needed which establishes the ethical basis and firm guiding principles which would underpin all subsequent secondary legislation, codes of conduct and guidance. In concrete terms, regulations should be used as the main means of placing these principles into practice for each specific area of animal use/concern. These could be supplemented, as necessary, by codes of conduct and guidance (in particular where extensive specialist input and/or further detailed guidance and interpretation for users are needed).

This approach will facilitate the inclusion of future international animal welfare standards (and subsequent improvements) as well as of additional areas where the welfare of animals needs to be re-codified.
It is important that these provisions do not remain static and fixed in time, but continue to be developed in response to the rapidly-occurring changes in our state of knowledge (including scientific progress) and evolving values on animal welfare.

The general principles reflected in the Animal Welfare Act should apply to national policy 'across the board', and so also be reverberated in other national policies which deal with issues affecting animals and their welfare.

There are also general requirements in relation to modern animal welfare legislation: This should be comprehensive and precise as well as clearly worded, progressive, powerful and forward-looking, efficacious and executable as well as adapted to the particular needs and challenges of the country in question. Dedication and commitment are certainly key factors which have to be firmly embedded in the new legislation as well, by manifesting an open-minded, ethically founded, compassionate and progressive approach to the subject along with the willingness of a government and a nation to accept their duties and responsibilities to their fellow beings.

Furthermore, the Animal Welfare Act should go beyond practical measures intended to improve the welfare of animals, and aim to develop a deeper and broader based humane ethic as well as a 'culture of caring' in society. This will be beneficial for society, people and animals.

II. ETHICAL GUIDING PRINCIPLES, OBJECTIVES AND TARGETS

Ethical Principles

This Model Animal Welfare Act will be based on the concept of a developing ethic of care and respect for animals throughout society; in terms of both practical care and protection of animals, and humane attitudes. This is considered an ethical imperative given present knowledge that the animals who share our world are living and sentient beings with an intrinsic value; and biologically determined natures, instincts and needs.

The main reasons for introducing animal welfare legislation should be grounded on this ethical approach. This means recognising and appreciating the need for reverence for life, and comprehensive practical care and protection. In cases where these ethical prerequisites are subjected to review — for example, in order to take account of the latest scientific evidence and/or important societal and economic needs — it is important that the authorities are clear about any potential impact on animal welfare (including relevant international and regional obligations), and are able to document any subsequent decision to override animal welfare considerations.

The lives of humans affect those of our fellow animals — both directly and indirectly — in many different ways. We know that animals experience pain and suffering, and that they have the potential to experience states of well-being. We also know that they have needs, interests and emotions which are important to them. Our actions can influence an animal's physical and psychological well-being; integrity and dignity as a creature; freedom; and even its life. Thus humans have a clear moral duty to provide for the welfare, and to protect the lives of other animals.

Animal welfare goes beyond the conservation of a species, as it includes care for the well-being of each individual animal in its own right. This is why the objective purpose and specific function of this Act is to protect all animals; meaning every animal as an individual without distinction. The single most important consideration in drafting any animal welfare law is its scope, and this Model AWA is no exception. As a forward-looking model, the authors have the responsibility to make this scope as far-reaching as possible. Yet we are hampered by the current state of science on the 'sentience' of individual animal species. We tend towards the view put forward in the 'The Cambridge Declaration on Consciousness' proclaimed on 7 July 2012, that many non-human animals share consciousness with humans. We also feel that as science progresses, far more animals will be shown to be sentient than has been imagined. In reality, all animals may well be sentient, but this will be difficult, if not impossible, to prove categorically. Thus, whilst it appears practical to restrict the scope of this Model AWA to sentient animals, we do not feel that this would do justice to the animals, as it will inevitably leave many sentient beings outside its scope and protection (whilst science plays 'catch-up' with actuality). Although the 'precautionary principle' can be applied theory, this is difficult to get right in practice (especially in enforcement and when needing proof in a court of law). We have, therefore, decided to include all animals within the scope of this Model AWA, but to grant particular emphasis and special care on sentient animals by focussing the sanctions (see Chapter 6) on sentient animals. (See also Section 2 and Section 4 of the Model AWA, plus corresponding Explanatory Notes).

Objectives and Targets

The introduction of modern animal welfare legislation enables a country to align its laws to international levels, including the incorporation of international and regional standards and provisions, ensuring international acceptance and regard. This can even present the opportunity to establish a new benchmark by realising a distinct and far-reaching improvement and advancement in the field of animal welfare.

An animal welfare law also provides an opportunity to prevent acts of animal cruelty and abuse, which diminish humans and can contribute to a violent and aggressive society. Indeed, a commitment to move away from animal cruelty to protect animal welfare is a statement reflecting the moral, cultural and social integrity and maturity of a nation and its people.

The proposal submitted here is designed as a precedent-setting framework law on a national level, giving the concrete outline of the statute which then will eventually find its substantive realisation on the tier of secondary (or so-called delegated or subordinate) legislation [and, as appropriate, codes of conduct and guidance]. In this manner, the law itself will contain general principles and 'core obligations'. This will ensure comprehensive legislation, with a coherent and consistent approach to animal welfare across all sectors. It will also ensure that animal welfare structures and general principles apply whilst detailed secondary legislation [and, as appropriate, codes of conduct and guidance] are being elaborated.

As stated above, in regard to secondary legislation it is recommended that regulations be used as the main means of placing these principles into practice for each specific area of animal use/concern. In addition to the power to introduce these detailed regulations, the individual sections will vest the Ministry or the competent Administration Authority (including Municipalities, where appropriate) with the warrant to issue codes of conduct and guidance to either regulate certain topics and areas of the relevant subject, set specific standards, or provide more detailed guidance for users and/or enforcement officers. Any secondary legislation, as well as codes and guidance, has to be drafted in consistency with the Act. This will avoid a proliferation of statutes, and provide a flexible approach whereby additional by-laws can be elaborated which complement and supplement the precepts. In this way the authorities can make amendments as opportune – for example, to take account of new scientific findings; changing societal attitudes and values; or the addition of international or regional standards or provisions which are of benefit to animals and need to be incorporated into national law. It will also make it possible to react swiftly to any new animal welfare challenges that might arise.

> Animal welfare goes beyond the conservation of a species, as it includes care for the well-being of each individual animal in its own right.

The moral values of a nation are supposed to be reflected in its legislation. However, it is recognised that in some countries the importance of animal welfare may not yet be ingrained in society. Moreover, improvement is needed even in countries where animal welfare is more highly prioritised. For these reasons, the ultimate ambition of this Act is to change this situation over time; through proactive measures to change the mind-set

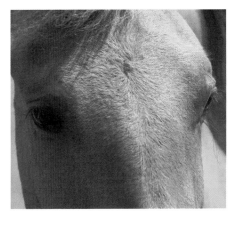

and ethic in the broad population to appreciate animals as sentient fellow-beings deserving of respect and care. Indeed, this change is needed to ensure the co-operation and support of the community for this new regulatory system providing for the welfare of animals.

Inclusion of animal welfare in the Criminal Code or Penal Code of a country might be considered a more impressive deterrent than a dedicated Animal Welfare Act. However, including all criminal offences against animals in one single body of law has a number of clear advantages. One dedicated Act will be comprehensive, compact and user-friendly. This is important as animal welfare legislation is not only addressed at the legal profession and government agencies, but also targets the general public as its main audience: They will have to conform to the law and thus will need to explicitly understand what is expected of them in this context.

This approach is in particular an option if no substantial animal welfare and protection provisions have already been introduced in a country, thus embedding new legal measures in this context might allow for a consolidated compendium of laws. If already a complex and detailed system of statutes including those with pertinent animal welfare relevance is in place, the Model AWA is aiming at complementing, supporting and strengthening the existing codes and regulations including any penalty schemes, especially in jurisdictions which permit the co-existence of penalties in various codes, i.e. for instance the animal welfare and penal codes. In this case usually a subsidiary clause would come into effect to warrant the *ne bis in idem* principle.

III. UPDATING FROM A 'PREVENTION OF CRUELTY TO ANIMALS' ACT

'Prevention of Cruelty to Animals' Acts Are Outdated and Inadequate

Some countries do not yet have any animal welfare legislation. Many others, particularly 'developing' countries, only have traditional 'Animal Protection' or basic 'Prevention of Cruelty to Animals' Acts. Some of these were introduced by former colonial powers, and often have not been revised since. These are now outdated and inadequate in terms of legal content, as well as ethical perspective. Although they provide basic protection against certain kinds of cruelty, mistreatment and (occasionally) neglect, they do not include an extensive legal set of principles or guidelines to safeguard animals from suffering and exploitation. They often do not include any prohibitions on the use of animals (for any purpose – no matter how harmful), no 'duty to care' for animals, nor any proactive provisions to develop an 'ethic of care'. In short, they are a narrow safety net designed to catch a limited range of specific acts of cruelty against animals (and often only a limited number of species of animals are covered). Furthermore, many sanctions can be deficient and penalties outdated, making even this safety net ineffective.

The Need for a More Comprehensive Approach to Animal Welfare Legislation

Over the years since these basic anti-cruelty laws were passed, a plethora of enhancements have changed the landscape of animal welfare legislation worldwide, sometimes in quite substantial ways. These have included not only a number of updated criteria concerning the ethical and moral foundations of animal welfare provisions and a very different perspective of the animal's position in society and in our lives; but also significant developments in animal welfare science and international policy. Within society, we have seen the progressive development of the sense of responsibility and willingness of populations to show compassion and care towards animals. These changes at various levels – individual, societal, ethical, scientific and political – have found expression in new laws providing a more considered, forward-looking, and comprehensive approach to animal welfare.

Even a summary comparison between these basic traditional 'Animal Protection' or 'Prevention of Cruelty to Animals' Acts, and some of the more modern and progressive animal welfare laws (for example, those of Austria, Germany, Croatia, New Zealand, Norway, Tanzania and the UK, to name just a few) illuminates the short-comings of the former. These inadequate and outdated laws simply fail to provide either a 'duty to care' governing human conduct or justice for our fellow animals.

There are other sound reasons, beyond changing values and international obligations, why countries with outdated animal protection or anti-cruelty laws are now seeking to replace these with modern, comprehensive animal welfare legislation. These include: international reputation, economic interests (e.g. to meet changing consumer and trade requirements), health (meeting human and animal health requirements), and protecting the country's fauna heritage (from exploitation and damage).

IV. PROPOSED NEW MEASURES FOR CONSIDERATION

Implementation of the Model Animal Welfare Act

As a discipline, animal welfare law is a relatively young sector of the law which is currently experiencing significant and far-reaching changes. This provides great scope for the introduction of new considerations and perspectives in order to influence the future development and execution of this field of juridical expertise. This means undertaking thorough research and analysis of all the different requirements linked to the field, as well as integrating the latest legal, policy, scientific, ethical and practical advancements. This Model Animal Welfare Act has followed this approach, seeking to spare busy legislators from some of this lengthy background research.

In order to introduce major improvements in their animal welfare legislation, countries will need vision, commitment (to doing what is just and right), courage (to break fresh ground) and endeavour (the hard work needed to pass and implement legislation).

The absolutely perfect 'model' law is – admittedly – not achievable. This Model Animal Welfare Act can be used as a guide, but it will need to be adapted to take account of each country's national situation (including its legislative procedures and provisions, socio-cultural situation, and specific animal welfare issues). However, with this approach countries will have the opportunity to design modern, comprehensive animal welfare legislation on a very high level.

Ideally, the recognition of an animal as an individual sentient being and the obligation to respect and protect animals as fellow-creatures should be firmly embedded within the entirety of the juridical system of every country.

The Constitution

This task should preferably commence with the embodiment of key principles and responsibilities in the respective constitutions (as are increasingly being introduced in many countries across the world), thus establishing the foundations for comprehensive and effective care and protection of the animal by the state.

At the very minimum, a constitutional provision on animal welfare and protection should include

- Recognition that animals are sentient beings with an intrinsic value;
- An explicit commitment/pledge of the Country/State/Government to prioritise animal welfare (as for instance a state objective); and
- Where a country has a federal system of government, recognition in the constitution that animal welfare legislation is a matter of federal legislative power.

The following further provisions are also highly recommended to be manifested in the constitution directly or otherwise at least on statutory level that

- Require the government and the citizens at all times to consider animals with respect, and treat them with compassion; safeguarding their welfare and protecting their intrinsic value;
- Require the government to introduce laws and enforcement structures so as to afford animals the highest level of care and protection; and
- Require the government to develop and support humane education programmes to encourage respect and compassion for people, animals and the environment, and the recognition of the interdependence of all living beings.

Policy

Another identified need is the early introduction of a national policy/strategy on animal welfare. This will provide the government with greater detail on the ethical basis of its animal welfare work, and chart a course that it can follow for the proactive development of measures to improve animal welfare and educate and inform stakeholders and citizens. The advantage of formulating an animal welfare policy/strategy at an early stage is that this clarifies the work that has to be undertaken by the government, so the necessary structures, systems and expertise can be developed to deal with this task (indeed, these will be needed before legislation can be considered and drafted, let alone implemented). Simultaneously setting goals, as well as a time-frame for reaching individual objectives under these, is imperative. Governments often attempt to draft animal welfare legislation before they have the necessary policy structures and expertise available, leading to inadvertent mistakes and ineffective provisions which subsequently require amendment.

The following would need to be incorporated in any animal welfare policy/strategy, as a minimum:

- **The Ethical Basis for Animal Welfare Policies/Laws**

Philosophical beliefs: including those based on science, culture, religion and societal values. Whereby recognition of sentience must be featured as a basic precept.

- **Any Regional or International Requirements**

Including the OIE's international animal welfare standards and any other applicable international or regional standards; agreements or provisions.

- **Future Plans for Animal Welfare Legislation**

Including plans to develop a modern, comprehensive framework act, supported by secondary legislation, and – as applicable – codes of conduct and guidance, including a timeframe for regular reviews. [Likewise, schemes to progressively develop animal welfare in key areas, following the 3Rs principles (for all uses of animals, not just experimentation), including the eradication of factory farming systems such as battery cages, veal crates, sow stalls, farrowing crates etc.]

- **Government Structures and Enforcement Systems**

Including plans to develop government structures and enforcement systems which are able to deal effectively with animal welfare policy administration and enforcement. This will need to identify the lead government department and bodies to be involved in enforcement; formulate plans to develop an effective animal welfare committee; establish what more is needed to strengthen systems, procedures and staffing – including expertise/training; and funding provisions for animal welfare policy, programmes, education and enforcement.

- **Knowledge and Skills on Animal Welfare**

Including plans to improve knowledge and skills on animal welfare where most needed, e.g.: drivers of change (including OIE Delegates and AW Focal Points), policy officials, enforcement officers, veterinarians, animal owners and keepers, farmers/farmers groups, traders, transporters and handlers. This would include building national animal welfare science programmes and capacity building/training and guidance for animal welfare; and could be carried out in conjunction with extension services, development partners and NGOs.

- Research and Development

Including the collection and dissemination of good practice: pilot projects, case studies and research (within and outside of the region) – thus facilitating the application of nationally appropriate best practice. This should include the collection and use of indigenous knowledge on animals and animal welfare. It would also include information on subjects such as the use of alternatives to animal experiments. Research conducted by independent scientists should be used, as opposed to research performed by scientists commissioned or funded by animal industries.

- Education and Awareness

Including the incorporation of humane education/animal welfare education into existing school programmes; the development of animal welfare in further and higher education (for example veterinary universities and agricultural colleges); and the development of clear consumer information, and communication and public awareness strategies for the broader public (including through mass media). This could incorporate the use of international days – such as World Animal Day, World Wildlife Day and World Rabies Day – for public awareness events and activities.

- Mainstreaming Animal Welfare

The integration of animal welfare into relevant sectoral and cross sectoral policies and programmes (including poverty reduction, livelihoods, agriculture and fisheries, transport, trade, science and research, health/safety; rabies control and environment).

- Monitoring and Evaluation

The establishment of systems for monitoring and evaluation of progress with the implementation of animal welfare legislation, including robust systems for monitoring compliance with animal welfare legislation (which would include OIE standards): Such systems to always be independent of animal industries, in order to avoid any conflict of interest. Also, mechanisms to monitor enforcement and collate feed-back on animal welfare problems (for corrective action on the root of problems). Plus systems and processes for the ongoing review of ethical, scientific and practical as well as also international developments in the field, and analysis of the policy and legislative enhancements needed to take account of these.

Competent Authority

One common fundamental problem is where to site the animal welfare remit, i.e. which government department should be given the lead responsibility for animal welfare? Traditionally, animal welfare is located within the Ministry of Agriculture. This arrangement can lead to a clash of interests, i.e. with animal welfare being pitted against competing interests being dealt with in the same department, such as: political, economic, production, land use, science/research etc. In such cases, there is a danger that animal welfare objectives would lose out to human-centred or economic considerations, regardless of any (more altruistic) moral imperative.

Therefore some animal welfare experts promote the idea of a separate ministry for animal welfare affairs. However, such a Ministry is probably more likely to have little power in government. Thus it may be preferable for a separate independent department to be created within a sympathetic ministry.

Another important consideration is where the necessary expertise resides. The OIE, which has now been accepted as the international lead organisation for animal welfare, has national Delegates from each of its member countries. These overwhelmingly come from the national Ministry of Agriculture/Veterinary Services. As animal health is an important component of animal welfare, veterinarians will have a strong professional interest in animal welfare.

So, a country may decide to site animal welfare in the Ministry of Agriculture. However, where this is done, it is essential that measures are taken to avoid any conflicts of interest or ethos.

Another question of competence which frequently arises is that of wildlife welfare. This is often sited under the Ministry of the Environment. In this case, there are (at least) two separate Ministries dealing with wildlife welfare and animal welfare more generally. This can create difficulties whereby different approaches to welfare are adopted by each Ministry, meaning that animals are treated differently depending on the category they fall under (wildlife and other, in this case – so, for example, game animals kept for farming may have much laxer welfare requirements than wild game/game kept in wildlife reserves). This is clearly not equitable, given the uniform ethical principles underlying animal welfare policy and law. It is preferable to have one department leading on animal welfare across the board, so it can establish sound and coherent welfare principles and policies for all animals, and build animal welfare expertise across the board. But if a country does decide to site wildlife welfare under a separate Ministry (e.g. Environment), then it needs to establish procedures to ensure a consistent humane ethos and practical approach in each Ministry.

Occasionally other aspects of animal welfare are sited under other Ministries – for example, live animal transport may be placed under a Ministry of Transport or animals used in science and research under a Ministry for Science and Technology. This raises similar concerns to those discussed above in relation to wildlife, and the same recommendations would apply.

Another option, which has been used by some countries, is to embed the animal welfare remit under a ministry that has no involvement with any animal issues (i.e. covers no issues involving the commercial exploitation of animals). For example, Denmark placed its animal welfare department under the Ministry of Justice at one stage, but this brought a problem with expertise (the practical result of which was that policy staff from the Ministry of Justice had to be supported by veterinary experts at relevant EU/Council of Europe animal welfare meetings). In this case, the remit has now been moved to the Danish Ministry of Food, Agriculture and Fisheries.

Each government will have to make its own choice from the above options, and this will depend largely on its existing government structures and seats of expertise. Situations, needs and practicalities will differ from country-to-country. However, it is paramount that the responsible government agency builds the political will, systems and procedures necessary to administer this important remit. This also means building the values, principles and expertise which will equip it to champion animal welfare throughout government.

The Ministry in charge of the remit will need to place substantial political importance and significance to this subject, and be prepared to allocate to it the necessary staff, resources and political support. It will need to ensure that it is viewed as a strong moral imperative, of value and relevance in its own right, and not a marginal issue to be disregarded when other (vested) interests are at stake. The officer in charge must be willing to dedicate considerable energy and commitment to the task, and to be a strong advocate for the cause, promoting this throughout government and society more broadly.

This is not so much a legal problem as a political and administrative one: Relatively easy to overcome if the political support and commitment is present.

Involved Parties

It should be noted that only legislation which is widely considered just and equitable can ultimately be enforceable and effective. Thus it would be advantageous to invite all stakeholders – who may be affected by the law in any way – to participate in consultations about this Act and any subsequent secondary legislation, [and codes of conduct and guidance]. The aim should be to provide all stakeholders with the opportunity to examine and discuss the legislation from the early stages of formulation, in order to eliminate any potential areas of conflict. Where feasible, consultations should include face-to-face meetings, as well as written representations, as this provides stakeholders with the opportunity to interact and gain an understanding of the (often competing) needs and interests of other groups of stakeholders.

There will be various categories of stakeholders and concerned parties which will need to be consulted by the legislative body right from the start of the decision-making process. These will include (but not be restricted to) the following:

- **Official Bodies**

This would include all relevant Ministries (the Lead Ministry should invite all who cover issues where animal welfare would be a consideration and others with a broader interest, such as the Ministry of Education and the Ministry of Justice) and the State Veterinary Services; enforcement authorities (such as the Police); and regional and local government (including Municipalities, which are often responsible for stray management work). *(The Veterinary Services are likely to be the leading official professionals in this field. The Police can be particularly challenged by the task of enforcing the law, and need to be involved and informed to develop their understanding and commitment to the task. The Ministry for Education, on the other hand, is relevant as regards the need for education and awareness; including the incorporation of animal welfare as an integral part of the national curriculum and its inclusion in relevant further and higher education courses.)*

- **Animal Professionals**

This would include veterinarians and other professionals working with animals, such as animal behaviourists and animal welfare scientists/researchers. Such professionals should be independent of animal use industries, to prevent any conflict of interest.

- **Trade/Industry Representatives**

Bodies representing commercial interests such as: farmers; breeders; fisheries; fish and meat product producers; transporters of live animals; slaughterhouses; animal research and testing bodies; companies using animals for shows, exhibitions, competitions, entertainment or leisure; users of animals for work; boarders; and shops and marketers of animals and animal products. (The latter would include supermarkets.)
The incorporation of trade/industry representatives ensures that the resultant legislation is practical. However, their representations should be taken in the context of their known vested interests, and carefully weighed against moral imperatives.
Other branches of industry which might only be touched indirectly by the consequences of the law should also be invited to take part in consultations – such as the tourist trade (which could profit from efficient animal welfare statutes enhancing the international repute of the country in this particular respect).

- **Non-Governmental Organisations**

This would include both animal welfare organisations (NGOs dealing specifically with animal welfare issues) and other NGOs working on broader issues related to animals (such as the environment, farming or development). Other NGOs may need to develop their understanding of animal welfare, and the legislative provisions, in order to ensure that their work takes account of this new dimension.

- **Consumer Groups**

This would include any relevant consumer interest groups.

- **The Public**

The public should be involved in any legislative consultations, as the Act confers certain obligations upon them (including a 'duty of care').

- **Animal Welfare Committee**

An Animal Welfare (and Ethics) Committee/Council should be formed at the earliest possible stage to assist the government during the process of compiling the content and wording of the law. This Committee/Council should consist of a proper balance of members from the fields of animal welfare, animal use, animal care, professionals (veterinarians and animal behaviourists) and scientific experts, as well as neutral representatives, including ethicists (it is vital that professional ethical expertise is utilised, and is recommended that ethical training is given to all members). Expertise from all animal welfare issues should also be called upon, and consideration given to constituting sub-groups for each major issue category.

Designation of the Law

Two alternative designations are suggested for a modern, comprehensive animal welfare law: either 'Animal Welfare Act' or 'Animal Protection Act'. In principle, both the terms 'animal protection' and 'animal welfare' signify that animals are afforded protection under the law. However, 'animal protection' puts the main emphasis on the element of protection, i.e. defence against endangerment, violence and assaults (including cruel treatment and acts that cause pain or suffering); whereas 'animal welfare' also incorporates the concept of care, consideration and circumspection with regard to the individual animal. 'Animal welfare' is about ensuring that an animal is in a state of overall well-being, which is a condition of physical, mental and emotional harmony and includes the ability to live naturally and to meet all species-specific and ethological needs. Thus, in our view, 'animal welfare' is the more comprehensive and attentive definition, with 'animal protection' regarded as an integral element of 'animal welfare'. Consequently, we feel the designation 'Animal Welfare Act' to be preferable as a more accurate, precise and suitable description (see Section 1 of the Model AWA). Alternatively, it would be considered absolutely acceptable to use the designation 'Animal Welfare and Protection Act'.

Another consideration is that accustomed terminology will differ from country-to-country. In countries where the concept is relatively new, the term 'animal welfare' is more common, deriving from the OIE and/or scientific work in this field. In other countries, either the term 'animal welfare' or the term 'animal protection' may have already evolved in popular use. However, another reason we have used the designation 'Animal Welfare Act' is because we feel it is more widely used and better reflects the current international policy and scientific environment.

Clearly the designation 'Prevention of Cruelty to Animals Act' would be unsatisfactory and misleading for a modern, comprehensive law.

Content of the Law

The legal target for a modern and progressive animal welfare law should be the regulation of all areas where humans have the potential to affect the lives or welfare of animals, ensuring their humane treatment and care. It should also cover the progressive development of a broader based humane ethic and 'culture of caring' in society.

To achieve this coverage, definitions are of utmost importance. Acts of commission, as well as omission, must be encompassed in the statutes. Also, a 'duty of care' has to be a prominent theme, reflecting the characteristics and requirements of individual animals.

Ideally, the Animal Welfare Act should, as a framework act, cover all aspects of animal welfare. In addition to general provisions covering all animals, this would include all major categories of animal issues:

- Companion animals (pets) – including stray dog and cat management;
- Animals kept for farming purposes – including fish farming – as well as animal transport and killing/slaughter;
- Animals used for experimentation – including science, research and testing;
- Wildlife – including 'pest' control, and animals in zoos/aquaria;
- Animals used for work; and
- Animals used for sports, leisure or entertainment.

It is important to include all aspects of animal welfare, even those which have been separately covered in the past (as is often the case with wildlife or stray management). This is because there must be a coherent and consistent approach to animal welfare across all sectors. The Model Animal Welfare Act has, therefore, established general guiding principles and rules ('core obligations') covering all areas of animal welfare.

The Animal Welfare Act will also vest the Ministry or Competent Authority with the powers to issue secondary legislation. This is particularly important for areas where specific animal welfare problems have been identified, or where abuse and infringements have been found.

In addition the Act will also warrant the Ministry or Competent Authority with the powers to enact supplementary codes of conduct and guidance to enable them to provide detailed guidance and interpretation for users and/or enforcement bodies, as necessary. This will give the relevant authorities the flexibility to meet new and emerging needs (for example, in response to new technologies which may affect animal welfare), and to provide any additional specialist input and advice considered necessary.

The powers to issue delegated legislation as well as supplementary provisions will not only cover specific areas of animal welfare concern, but also major areas of work needed to develop a broader based humane ethic and 'culture of caring' in society.

These would include

- Development of knowledge and skills on animal welfare issues (including training/capacity building and guidance);
- Development of education (including programmes in schools, further and higher education) and public awareness;
- Research and development work for animal welfare (including animal welfare research; and the collection and dissemination of good practice); and
- Development, support, promotion and encouragement of non-profit animal welfare organisations.

Ideally, this Act should supersede or take precedence over all other legislation with which it may conflict. However, particular care should be taken to ensure that: it provides for the introduction of higher level provisions in the future (for example, to meet international standards, and/or to upgrade animal welfare standards following scientific or ethical advances); does not supersede any laws or provisions which provide greater protection for animal welfare; and will not conflict with any existing constitutional provisions.

It is recommended that a review is carried out of all other Acts and laws involving animal issues, to ensure that there is conformity and a solid platform for a progressive approach. This review should identify all laws that require amendment and/or where provisions should be repealed and integrated into the Animal Welfare Act. Acts which may need revision, rather than combination, would include measures covering areas such as animal health and disease control (which may impact on animal welfare, but be directed at other specific purposes).

Structure and Segmentation of the Law

The structure and composition of animal welfare laws worldwide vary greatly, with diverse priorities, perspectives and approaches. As already addressed briefly in Section II, this present suggestion is based on the concept of a framework law which establishes the ethical basis and firm guiding principles which would underpin all subsequent subordinate or secondary legislation. The framework law should provide overall 'guiding principles' for animal welfare, and also identify core animal welfare issues which need to be regulated, establishing guiding principles for each issue. Then, it should supply the powers for the authorities to enact these principles in secondary legislation [and, as appropriate, 'Welfare Codes', standards and guidance].

It is recommended that detailed substantive provisions are dealt with in regulations, supplemented by 'Welfare Codes', standards and guidance whenever necessary. For this purpose no additional legislative measures are needed, as all these aforementioned aspects would be covered by the power directly delegated to the Ministry or

Competent Authority respectively through the Animal Welfare Act itself.

It is essential that any 'Welfare Codes' and standards are developed in accordance with the Animal Welfare Act, and any breach of these is taken to be a breach of the subject Act. Thus it is imperative that any Welfare Codes and standards (or amendments to these) are disseminated and well publicised. It should be borne in mind that 'Welfare Codes' and standards may be developed and amended outside of parliamentary processes, and thus the use of these should be restricted to matters of clarification and detail, with regulations being used in preference. Guidance notes should be considered a more informal source of advice and interpretation, and not be used when any legally binding provisions are required or desired.

Within the law, the ethical values and guiding principles the Act is drawing upon should precede the general rules (or 'core obligations') concerning the welfare and protection of animals, i.e. the basic precepts of the human-animal relation. In turn, these general rules should precede the rules relating to the specific issues/areas of concern identified. Thus, there is a clear distinction between the establishment of underlying principles, fundamental provisions and specific statutory provisions.

In practice, the purpose of the Act, its ideology, scope, intent, objectives and definitions would be found in 'Chapter 1: Preliminary Provisions'. This chapter would first and foremost contain the 'Title', then the 'Objectives' as well as the State's/Government's 'Support for Animal Welfare', the 'Scope of Application' and the 'Definitions'. This affords the opportunity to not only outline the law's purpose and mission but to also highlight its relevance as well as its concrete significance within the legal system itself. The 'Preliminary Provisions' provide above all the foundation for the Act; and thus they also constitute the basis for all the ensuing provisions.

The second chapter, entitled: 'Chapter 2: General Provisions' would comprise the statutes which are linked to human conduct towards animals in general, and normally are with a few exceptions addressed to 'everybody' and not coupled with any further specific preconditions. These concern, in particular, certain completely unacceptable acts of cruelty which thus should be particularly emphasised/highlighted. They cover: 'Prohibition of Cruelty to Animals', 'Prohibited Interventions Performed on Animals', 'Prohibition of Killing Animals', 'Prohibition of Passing on, Selling, Offering for Sale, Purchasing or Possessing Certain Animals (Doomed Animals)' and 'Obligation to Grant First Aid'.

The third chapter entitled: 'Chapter 3: Keeping of Animals/Care of Animals' would codify specific requirements which have to be fulfilled (as opposed to the more basic aspects of the human-animal relationship mentioned above). The scope of these requirements covers the care and protection of animals kept within a person's sphere of influence, custody or control in order to meet the need to care for the welfare of the individual animal in this state of dependence. In this situation, the explicit 'duty of care' (for the owner, keeper or person in charge of the animal) and the 'Five Freedoms' are of utmost importance, given human ethical responsibilities (for details see Part 1, I. Introduction). Still, access into these statutes of Chapter 3 shall preferably be sought more with regard to the 'principles of proper animal keeping' and not so much via the virtue of 'ownership' or the feature of being a 'person in charge of an animal'. Indeed, as perceptions of animals evolve over time, with increased emphasis on their intrinsic value and autonomy, the concept of 'ownership' of an animal becomes less ethical and acceptable, and human responsibilities for understanding and meeting animal needs as an act of 'guardianship' gain prominence.

Chapter 3 would be split into two distinct groups, 'A. General Regulations' and 'B. Special Regulations': The first group would determine the general or overall regulations to be observed for animals in human custody and care; and the latter would stipulate further parameters in the context of people's conduct towards animals, i.e. keeping animals within the scope of business activities, transport of animals, killing/slaughter etc.

Chapter 4 would cover specific categories of animal use. This enables separate provisions to be delineated covering concrete areas of animal use, meaning these can be tailored to conditions prevailing in the particular sector.

Chapter 5 would be devoted to the 'Enforcement and Execution Provisions' of the Act. This would include aspects such as: enforcement/implementation structures and systems; powers; and the allocation of responsibilities (including the Competent Authority, enforcement responsibilities, and also animal welfare organisations and the Animal Welfare (and Ethics) Committee).

Chapter 6 would be dedicated to the 'Penal and Final/Concluding Provisions'. This would include provisions covering both penal and administrative fines.

An ethically-based, comprehensive and future-orientated concept of animal welfare should be overarching, and cover all animals indiscriminately. However, as special consideration and care is afforded to the welfare of sentient non-human animals, and in the interests of effective and practical enforcement, the sanctions focus on sentient animals (which would, based on current scientific knowledge, encompass all vertebrates, birds, fish and many other creatures, including cephalopods and decapod crustaceans; and through the application of the precautionary principle, any other animal which appears to be sentient).

Some animal welfare laws incorporate aspects of punishment/sanctions directly into provisions detailing the requirements of the law (and any related offence), i.e. the consequences of the breach are explicitly specified directly following the provision outlining each potential breach of the law. At face value this might seem quite practical as regards the application of the law. However, this would be at the expense of the general clarity and accessibility of the Act in question. This is firstly because continuous repetitions would make the text lengthy and unwieldy; and secondly because it would prove difficult to make comparisons between the consequences of different infringements.

Thus, preference is given to an arrangement which gathers all the consequences of infringements in a separate section of the legislative text, which would cover a number of violations: This approach has the advantage of streamlining the law and facilitating assessment of the impacts of individual provisions.

A banding system has been suggested for the establishment of fines. This is preferred to the establishment of fines in given units of currency, which tends to result in the level of fines being eroded by inflation as they become outdated (often combined with the reluctance to review the Act to update these). The value of fine bandings can be established by regulation, making it possible to update fine levels across the board by a simple regulatory amendment to take account of inflationary pressures. This system has the advantage of keeping the same differential between the level of fines (between different Acts, as well as within the same Act); as well as being simple administratively.

Another aspect that was briefly mentioned under Part 1, II. Ethical Guiding Principles, Objectives and Targets, above, which should be addressed in more detail here:

To some extent relevant criminal offences will already exist in the country's Penal or Criminal Code (as appropriate). To harmonise the provisions and to secure an identical approach one might want to consider either amending the Penal/Criminal Code accordingly, i.e. remove the criminal offences from the Penal/Criminal Code and add them to the Animal Welfare Act, or to redraft the latter to only deal with acts categorised as administrative offences.

However, in these cases discretion is needed, as the provisions of a new Animal Welfare Act should always be in addition to and not in lieu of any other laws protecting animals and animal welfare. Therefore certain penalty schemes shall be allowed to coexist in order to guard against weakening the position of animals and animal welfare in an already sophisticated legal system.

Certainly in cases where the country's Penal/Criminal Code does not already cover relevant criminal offences against animals it is considered preferable to include criminal offences, along with administrative offences, in one dedicated Animal Welfare Act. This is because although inclusion in the Criminal Code/Penal Code might, at first sight, be considered a more effective deterrent, there are clear advantages in including all offences in one single body of law. Probably the most important of these is the clarity and accessibility of having one compact compendium of animal welfare law; which is readily accessible to a wide range of potential users. This would include government agencies, the legal profession and animal welfare organisations which will all have to apply the law, and animal users as well as owners, keepers and handlers who will have to conform to the law – and all of these will need to understand exactly what is expected of them in this context. Indeed, providing all relevant provisions in one Act at the same time gives clarity around those bodies that have enforcement powers under the Act. Also, consistency of approach is easier when all offences are consolidated in one law – including the option of giving fines as well as prison sentences for both infringements and crimes, depending on the relative severity of the breach of the law.

Finally, it has to be highlighted that any law concerning the welfare and protection of animals should be a set of rules that are not primarily directed at the authorities alone, but also (and predominantly) aimed at the public and other interested parties including (but not limited to) animal businesses and industries; and animal welfare organisations (see Part 1, II. Ethical Guiding Principles, Objectives and Targets, above for a fuller list of potential stakeholders). Therefore it should be comprehensive, and also straightforward, accessible and easily manageable for every citizen. Thus the approach used here has ensured that the Model Animal Welfare Act is clearly drafted, tightly structured, logically ordered, and well elaborated – beginning with a table of contents for user-friendly navigation.

PART 2

Proposal for the Wording of a New Animal Welfare Act

An Act to provide for the protection of the lives and welfare of animals, recognition of their sentience and intrinsic value, and the progressive development of a broader based humane ethic and 'culture of caring' in society. This Act is based on internationally accepted moral and scientific principles for animal welfare and includes: humane treatment and care; the prohibition of cruelty; the development of animal welfare structures, procedures and controls; and education and awareness.

CHAPTER 1: PRELIMINARY PROVISIONS

Section 1 — Title, Commencement and Conflicting Provisions

This Act may be cited as the 'Animal Welfare Act'. [It shall come into effect on such date as the Minister may appoint, by notice published in the gazette.]

This Act will supersede or take precedence over all other legislation with which it may conflict, unless such legislation provides a higher level of protection for the welfare of an animal.

Section 2 — Objectives

The aim of this Act is the protection of the lives and welfare of all animals, and the development of humankind's respect and moral responsibility for our fellow creatures. This aim includes the progressive development of humane attitudes throughout society, as well as practical measures to protect the welfare of animals and provide a clear 'duty of care' for all citizens.

Each animal is recognised as an individual, with an intrinsic value and a life which matters. Sentient animals are afforded special care and consideration to protect their welfare, as they are recognised as having biologically determined natures, instincts, emotions and needs which matter to them; as well as the ability to experience pain and to suffer.

Section 3 — Support for Animal Welfare

(1) The state is obliged to promote and support animal welfare, and the development of a humane ethic, in all areas/sectors whereby it has the authority and the duty to educate, inform, make the public sensitive to animal welfare issues, as well as to support the implementation of animal welfare legislation.

(2) Such promotion and support shall include, but not be limited to, animal welfare and humane attitudes in: scientific research; legal information and capacity-building; educational programmes; competent authority and enforcement capacity-building; rural development and animal welfare-friendly keeping systems; and public awareness activities. Public awareness activities shall include, but not be limited to, consumer awareness, and shall be supported by state action to ensure full and accurate marketing and labelling of any products the purchase or choice of which could have animal welfare implications. It shall also include the dissemination of animal welfare information and advice in veterinary, para-veterinary, agricultural extension, development, legal and environmental work.

Section 4   Scope of Application

This Act applies to all non-human animals. Chapters 5 and 6, on enforcement and penalties, only apply to sentient animals. It is prohibited to exempt any animal from the coverage of this Act, and any sentient animal from its associated penalties.

Section 5   Definitions

For the purpose of this Act, the following terms shall have the meaning as detailed below:

1. **Animal:** Any mammal, bird, reptile, amphibian, fish, insect or other multi-cellular organism that is not a plant or fungi.
2. **Animal Protection:** The act of protecting the lives or well-being of animals, including safeguarding animals from cruel treatment and acts that cause the animal harm, injury, loss, pain, suffering or fear and distress.
3. **Animal Sanctuary:** A facility which cares for abused, neglected, unwanted, or otherwise vulnerable animals, protecting them for the rest of their lives in conditions as close as possible to the relevant species' natural habitat. Unlike animal shelters, sanctuaries do not aim to rehome animals, and unlike wildlife rehabilitation centres, do not aim to release rehabilitated animals back into the wild. The term 'Animal Sanctuary' can only be used where the facility in question is operated by a charitable, non-profit animal welfare organisation.
4. **Animal Shelter:** A facility to house and keep abandoned, rescued, unwanted, lost or homeless animals which safeguards their well-being and provides necessary care and attention until the animals can be reunited with their owners, adopted or rehomed. The term 'Animal Shelter' can only be used where the facility in question is operated by a charitable, non-profit animal welfare organisation.
5. **Animal Welfare:** How an animal is coping with the conditions in which he/she is living. For animal welfare to be satisfactory, the animal must be in a state of overall well-being, which is a condition of physical, mental and emotional harmony, and which includes the ability to live naturally and to meet all species-specific and ethological needs: This would include the provision of the Five Freedoms under Section 6 (3) 1.
6. **Animal Welfare Inspector:** A professionally qualified and competent officer appointed by the Competent Authority to execute the subject Act.
7. **Commercial Companion Animal Breeder:** Any person
    1) Breeding companion animals in a location other than a family home; or
    2) Having more than three unsterilised female animals in their home, any of which is used for the purposes of breeding which breed two or more litters in any 12 month period.
8. **Companion Animal (or 'Pet'):** Any domesticated animal socialised and commonly kept, cared for, or possessed by humans within the sphere of the household for companionship, pleasure, protection or personal assistance.
9. **Competent Authority:** The regulatory authority that has the legally delegated or vested authority, capacity, or power to perform the designated functions.
10. **Domestic Animal:** Any animal of a species that has been tamed or selectively bred over many generations and kept by humans for companionship, food, fibre, or work; including those that have been abandoned or gone astray.
11. **Euthanasia:** A procedure to put an animal to death painlessly in order to relieve suffering from a terminal illness or incurable condition. The method used should involve minimal restraint and stress for the animal.
12. **Farmed Animal:** Any domestic or wild animal which is normally kept and raised on farms, and is kept for the production of any animal products (i.e. food, feed, fur, feathers, leather, skin, wool and fibre) or for the breeding of animals for such production.
13. **Game Animal:** A land mammal or bird, either in the wild or farmed, which is hunted for sport or food, and is

not normally considered to be a domestic animal.

14. **Humane Killing:** A procedure which induces either the instantaneous death of an animal or which uses stunning or anaesthetisation that renders the animal unconscious and insensible until death supervenes. In both cases, this must be accomplished with the absence of pain, suffering, fear or distress; including during the period of induction of unconsciousness, where this is not immediate. 'Humane Killing' implies the use of appropriate measures/methods and suitable tools/means or equipment, applied by operators with the necessary training and expertise.

15. **Intervention:** Any procedure resulting in damage to or the loss of a sensitive part of the body or the alteration of the bone structure.

16. **Keeper:** Any person who is responsible for the animal, its health and well-being either on a permanent or on a temporary basis or has an animal in (his/her) care or under (his/her) supervision/control.

17. **Minister/Ministry:** The Minister/Government Department in charge of the government department which has been specified as responsible for the animal welfare remit in question. *Factors to consider in this regard are discussed at paragraph IV. 1. above.*

18. **'Pest' Animal:** An animal with characteristics that humans deem to be damaging or unwanted.

19. **Pet Shop:** Any mercantile establishment or enterprise where companion animals (pet animals) can be purchased, including both premises and 'virtual' or online sales, but excluding animal shelters and pounds.

20. **Pound:** A place where stray animals may be officially taken and kept until claimed by their owners.

21. **Precautionary Principle:** A precautionary or cautious approach which must be taken in the interests of animal welfare for each and every case where an action, policy or provision has a suspected risk of causing damage or harm to an animal or its welfare, in the absence of scientific consensus that the action, policy or provision is not detrimental.

22. **Ritual and/or Religious Slaughter:** The slaughter of animals for the production of specially prepared foods, mostly for Kosher and Halal meats in the Jewish and Muslim traditions, respectively. The prescribed method involves throat cutting, allowing the blood to drain out, causing the animal's death. *[Some religious traditions permit reversible (non-fatal) pre-stunning, whereas others do not permit any stunning. Slaughter by bleeding without pre-stunning has been found to impair welfare, and thus may be banned or severely restricted. There are also a number of other requirements which must be met in order for slaughter to comply with Jewish or Muslim rite. However, an animal welfare law is not the place to establish such religious criteria.]*

23. **Sentience:** The capacity to perceive or feel things. Sentient beings share with us consciousness, feelings, emotions, perceptions – and the ability to experience pain, suffering, fear, distress and states of well-being.

24. **Slaughter:** The killing of an animal for the purpose of the production of meat, food and/or other animal products and by-products.

25. **Stray:** Any domestic animal (most commonly dogs or cats) not under direct control by a person or not prevented from roaming.
    There are three types of stray dogs/cats:
    1) Free-roaming owned – not under direct control of, or restriction by, a person/owner at a particular time;
    2) Free-roaming with no owner or keeper; and
    3) Feral – a domestic dog/cat having returned to an untamed state from domestication, in particular after escape from captivity or after abandonment.

26. **Stunning:** A process which, when applied to an animal, causes immediate loss of consciousness which lasts until death.

27. **Trap:** Any device or enclosure that is designed to close upon, hold fast, confine, or otherwise capture an animal, whether or not the device or enclosure results in capture.

28. **Veterinarian:** A person who has successfully graduated from a recognised faculty of veterinary medicine and is officially registered, certified or licensed to practice as a veterinarian.

29. **Wild Animal:** Any animal with the exception of a domestic, companion, stray or feral animal.

30. **Wildlife Rehabilitation Centre:** A facility for receiving injured, ill/diseased, abused, orphaned, rescued or

domesticated wildlife for caring and treatment in order to restore former health and capacities and to subsequently secure the release into a sustainable safe natural environment.

31. **Zoological Garden (Zoo):** A park or an institution, which must be accredited by the World Association of Zoos and Aquaria (WAZA), in which living animals are kept in captivity and usually exhibited to the public.

This is not a comprehensive list of definitions. For example, it could be extended to include some more abstract and ambiguous terms such as

- *Intrinsic – The inherent value of something independent of its worth (or usefulness) to anybody, or anything, else; or*
- *Well-being – A multidimensional state that includes indicators from three broad criteria:*
  - *A high level of biological functioning.*
  - *Freedom from suffering (in the sense of fear, pain, distress and other negative experiences).*
  - *Positive experiences such as comfort and contentment. It is part of good animal welfare, along with fitness.*

Following the guiding principles of the five freedoms, important contributory factors to well-being could be said to include: The absence of pain, suffering, injury, disease and discomfort as well as of fear and distress; the freedom from thirst, hunger and malnutrition as well as the freedom to express normal behaviour and exercise all somatic functions.

Section 6   Fundamental Principles of Animal Welfare

(1) Based on the objectives mentioned in Section 2 of this Act, the State and all citizens must recognise animals as beings with an intrinsic value and a life which matters; and sentient beings as having biologically determined natures, instincts, emotions and needs which matter to them; as well as the ability to experience pain and to suffer.

(2) Animal welfare is an important aspect of any developed society, and reflects the degree of moral and cultural maturity of that society. Humans therefore have a moral responsibility to respect, protect and care for animals; ensuring their welfare to the greatest extent practicable. This 'duty of care' should be reflected in any implementing regulations (and Welfare Codes', standards and guidance), and human moral responsibilities codified.

(3) In order to give effect to the fundamental principles of this Animal Welfare Act, every person exercising powers under, applying or interpreting it and any regulations (supplemented when necessary by 'Welfare Codes', standards and guidance) shall have regard to

1. The internationally recognised 'Five Freedoms', which are included in the OIE's 'Guiding Principles' for Animal Welfare:
   1) Freedom from Hunger and Thirst and Malnutrition – by ready access to fresh water and a diet to maintain full health and vigour;
   2) Freedom from Physical and Thermal Discomfort – by providing a suitable environment including shelter and a comfortable resting area;
   3) Freedom from Pain, Injury and Disease – by prevention or rapid diagnosis and treatment;
   4) Freedom to Express Normal Patterns of Behaviour – by providing sufficient space, proper facilities and company of the animal's own kind; and
   5) Freedom from Fear and Distress – by ensuring conditions and treatment which avoid mental suffering.
2. The internationally recognised 'Three Rs', which should be applied to all commercial uses of animals, particularly where there are any doubts that the welfare needs of animals can be met:
   1) Reduction in numbers of animals;
   2) Refinement of methods (and situations) of animal use; and
   3) Replacement of animals with non-animal alternatives and techniques.

(4) Where there is any doubt that an animal's welfare needs can be met, then the 'precautionary principle' must be

applied, and the animal's welfare given precedence.

(5) Where the needs of any particular species cannot be met in captivity, then no animal of that species must be kept (unless for a duration necessary to ensure the animal's welfare).

(6) The different purposes for which animals are kept and used must be regularly re-evaluated in the light of current scientific knowledge and prevalent societal morals and ethical values.

CHAPTER 2: GENERAL PROVISIONS

Section 7   Prohibition of Cruelty to Animals

(1) It is prohibited to inflict or cause pain, suffering or injury on any animal, or to expose them to fear or distress, or illness or disease, without sound justification *(based on over-riding reasons of animal and/or human welfare)*. It is furthermore prohibited, being the owner or person responsible, to cause or permit any animal to be so treated; or for any person to fail to take reasonable steps to prevent such treatment.

(2) Without limiting sub-section (1), sub-section (1) is in particular violated if a person

1. Kills any animal using a method which is inhumane, or in a manner that involves pain, suffering, injury, fear or distress for the animal.
2. Severs a limb from a live animal.
3. Wounds, beats, kicks, over-rides, over-drives, over-loads, overworks, mutilates, torments, tortures or otherwise treats any animal in a way that subjects, or is likely to subject, it to pain, suffering, injury, fear or distress.
4. Demands from an animal any work, labour or performance which is beyond the animal's current natural strength or species-specific behaviour, or of which the animal is physically or health-wise not capable at that time or which involves, or is likely to involve, pain, suffering, injury, fear or distress for the animal.
5. Does or omits to do an act with the result that pain, suffering, injury, fear, distress, illness or disease, is caused, or is likely to be caused, to an animal.
6. Fails to provide an animal he or she keeps or cares for with sufficient, appropriate and constantly accessible food and drink to maintain it in full health and vigour.
7. Offers an animal food or substances the ingestion or digestion of which causes, or is likely to cause, pain, suffering, injury, fear or distress for the animal; or forces the animal to ingest food and substances when this is not necessary due to reasons of the animal's health or on veterinary/medical grounds.
8. Fails to provide an animal he/she keeps or cares for with an appropriate environment including shelter, proper facilities, a comfortable resting area and the opportunity to carry out normal, non-harmful social behaviours, in a way that results, or is likely to result, in pain, suffering, injury, fear distress, or illness for the animal involved. In the case of an animal being exhibited to the public, this would include a place where the animal has the opportunity to seek privacy from the viewing public at all times.
9. Exposes an animal to temperatures, weather conditions, wrong chemistry (for aquatic animals), lack of oxygen or restriction of free movement inflicting, or likely to inflict, pain, suffering, injury, fear, distress, illness or disease on the animal.
10. Keeps or confines any animal in any enclosure, cage or other receptacle which is not designed in such a way, or does not measure sufficient in height, length and breadth, to permit the animal appropriate opportunity for movement and performance of its species-specific needs and behaviours, or does not provide access to a natural substrate, (unless this is a temporary measure to safeguard the animal's welfare).
11. Keeps any animal chained or tethered in a way that does not permit the animal appropriate opportunity for movement and performance of its species-specific needs and behaviours (unless this is a temporary measure to safeguard the animal's welfare).
12. Breeds animals which will be, or are likely to be, inflicted with pain, suffering, injury, fear, distress, illness

or disease; or where their descendants will be, or are likely to be, inflicted with pain, suffering, injury, fear, distress, illness or disease (inhumane breeding practices).

13. Raises an animal in a way that causes, or is likely to cause, them pain, suffering, injury, fear, distress, illness or disease, including subjecting the animal to premature maternal separation, based on the natural age of dispersion of the species.

14. Trains, promotes, stimulates or increases aggressiveness or fighting readiness of an animal through breeding selection or other breeding technologies or methods.

15. Advertises, imports, exports, keeps, possesses, sells, offers for sale, or passes on an animal bred, raised or treated in the ways referred to in items 12, 13 or 14 of this sub-section.

16. Sets an animal on another animal; incites animal fighting or causes an animal to fight against another animal or human; organises, assists or attends the fighting of any animal; owns, possesses, trains, transports, or sells any animal with the intent that such animal shall be engaged in fighting with another animal or human; keeps, uses, manages or assists in the management of any premises or place used for the purpose or partly for the purpose of fighting any animal, or permits any premises or place to be so kept, managed or used for the same; promotes or advertises any event involving animal fighting; or receives or causes or procures any person to receive any money or other valuable for the admission of any person to such premises or place or for the purpose of betting on or assisting at such fights; or possesses, whether for sale or self-use, video images of such fights.

17. Promotes, stimulates or increases aggressiveness/fighting readiness of an animal by training, 'negative reinforcement' or other similar methods.

18. Uses any measures, methods, aids or devices in training or during sports or competitions or similar events which are linked to pain, suffering, injury, fear or distress for an animal; or administers any unauthorised substance or drug in order to enhance an animal's performance. This shall include the prohibition of 'negative reinforcement' methods of training; and a ban on the use of any cruel devices and implements such as bullhooks, electric prods, goads, pitchforks, baseball bats, whips, and any other cruel devices.

19. Causes, procures or assists at any shooting or hunting event, match or competition wherein an animal   is released from captivity for the purpose of such event, match or competition; or receives or causes or procures any person to receive any money for such event, match or competition.

20. Uses any unauthorised devices or methods of capture or entrapment; or uses authorised traps and catching devices in such a way that does not result in capturing the animal unharmed or killing the animal instantly.

21. Uses a live animal for feed or bait, or breeds or keeps a live animal for this purpose. *[In cases where the welfare of animals cannot be assured without feeding with live feed or bait, then such animals shall not be kept.]*

22. Conveys or carries, whether in or upon any vehicle or not, any animal in such a manner or position which causes, or is likely to cause, pain, suffering, injury, fear, distress, illness or disease.

23. Abandons a domestic or companion animal; abandons or releases into the wild a non-indigenous wild animal; or abandons or releases into the wild an indigenous wild animal which has not been fully rehabilitated to adapt to a life in the wild or where there is any doubt that it will survive in the territory to which it is being released.

24. Gives an animal away as, or offers an animal as, a prize or award.

25. Uses an animal for film shots, advertising, exhibitions or similar purposes or events if this causes, or is likely to cause, pain, suffering, injury, fear, distress, illness or disease for the animal.

26. Performs/carries out an action of a sexual nature on or with an animal.

Section 8   Prohibited Interventions Performed on Animals

(1) Any intervention carried out on an animal other than for therapeutic or diagnostic purposes (in accordance with legal regulations applicable) is prohibited.

(2) It is in particular prohibited

1. To partly or completely amputate any body part;
2. To partly or completely remove or destroy any organ or tissue of the animal; or
3. To carry out any intervention to create a transgenic animal.

(3) Exceptions to these prohibitions are only permitted

1. To prevent reproduction;
2. To indicate a neutered stray animal by the tipping of an ear; or
3. When necessary for over-riding animal welfare reasons; and in such cases, only when there is no alternative solution and the most humane method available has been used.

(4) If the intervention will cause, or is likely to cause, any pain for the animal and in the cases referred to in sub-sections (3) 1. and (3) 2. above, it must be carried out under effective anaesthesia and by a veterinarian, who shall ensure that all available measures are taken to achieve a procedure and recovery free from pain, suffering, fear or distress, in particular including the administration of sedation, local anaesthesia, non-steroidal anti-inflammatory drugs and analgesia.

(5) It is prohibited to mark or identify an animal in such a way that causes, or is likely to cause, pain, suffering, injury, fear or distress.

(6) In addition: Authorisation of the Minister responsible, the Ministry or the Competent Authority to adopt any regulations [and establish, as appropriate, 'Welfare Codes', standards and guidance] in this context.

Section 9   Prohibition of Killing to Animals

(1) It is prohibited to kill an animal without any sound justification.

(2) It is prohibited to kill a companion animal, such as a dog or cat, for the purpose of obtaining/manufacturing food, feed, fur or other products.

(3) It is prohibited to kill any animal in order to provide entertainment or as part of a cultural ritual or celebration.

(4) Where authorisation is granted for the killing of vertebrate animals for any purpose covered in this Act *(for example, humane euthanasia of companion animals and the expert/competent killing of farm or game animals)*, this must be carried out in a specified humane manner, in accordance with Section 20 below.

(5) In addition: Authorisation of the Minister responsible, the Ministry or the Competent Authority to adopt any regulations [and establish, as appropriate, 'Welfare Codes', standards and guidance] in this context.

Section 10   Prohibition of Passing on, Selling, Offering for Sale, Purchasing or Possessing Certain Animals (Doomed Animals)

(1) It is prohibited to pass on, sell, offer for sale, transport or purchase any animal for whom the continuation of life would be connected with irremediable pain, suffering, agony, torment or distress for any other purpose than for its immediate euthanasia. Anybody acquiring or purchasing such an animal has to immediately euthanise, or ensure the immediate euthanasia of, the animal.

(2) It is furthermore prohibited to possess any animal, without reasonable cause, which is suffering irremediable pain, agony, torment or distress.

Section 11   Obligation to Grant First Aid

(1) Every person has, to the extent he/she can reasonably be expected to do so, to grant/render any animal in an accident, during common danger, or injured or in distress the necessary first aid and care, or, if this is not possible, to make all reasonable endeavours to arrange for such first aid and care and/or for appropriate diagnosis and treatment without delay.

(2) The owner or keeper of an animal is obliged to provide any sick, injured or distressed animal with diagnosis and appropriate treatment without any delay; where necessary, veterinary advice must be sought and followed.

CHAPTER 3: KEEPING OF ANIMALS/CARE OF ANIMALS

A. General Regulations

Section 12   Principles of Keeping Animals

(1) The owner or keeper of any animal is obliged to

1. Provide food and drink which is sufficient, accessible and appropriate to maintain the animal in full health and vigour and meet its physiological and ethological needs;

2. Provide the animal with satisfactory hygiene and care, including regular inspections and appropriate and humane management and handling; ensuring the promotion of good human-animal relationships and the absence of pain, suffering, injury, fear or distress for the animal;

3. Keep the animal in such a way that its physical functions and its behaviour are not disturbed or affected; and its ability to adapt is not overstrained or overtaxed;

4. Provide the animal with an appropriate environment, which meets its physiological and behavioural needs, including freedom of movement and appropriate social contacts and interaction (taking into consideration the species, age and degree of development, and domestication of the animal), and also to rapidly investigate any signs of stereotypical behaviour, as an indication that the animal's needs are being frustrated, and take remedial action without delay;

5. Provide the animal with appropriate shelter, facilities, and a comfortable resting area; always ensuring that the animal is not exposed to adverse temperatures, weather conditions, or lack of oxygen; and

6. When housing or confining an animal, ensure in particular that the space (including height, as well as floor space); condition of the ground/base; structural equipment of the buildings and facilities; the climate, including temperature, air circulation, natural light and ventilation; and noise level will safeguard the welfare of the animal and enable it to meet its physiological and behavioural needs.

(2) A person shall not manufacture, keep in stock, sell, offer for sale, deliver, or in any manner make use of any animal housing system, unless such a system conforms to the above welfare requirements for the keeping of animals, and any prescribed minimum standards established by the Competent Authority.

(3) It is prohibited to keep any animal permanently or prevalently chained or tethered.

(4) Wild animals must in no case be kept chained or tethered, even temporarily, unless this is to prevent imminent danger – for example, in an emergency situation; and dogs should not be tethered more than momentarily or on a running chain which enables free movement and exercise (for purposes of management or control).

(5) Any person keeping a domestic animal shall ensure that the animal is inspected and attended to at least once a day or more depending on the species' particular needs.

(6) In case of any ownership dispute concerning an animal or animals, the outcomes shall be decided (e.g. by the civil courts) taking into account the best interests of the individual animal or animals.

(7) In addition: Authorisation of the Minister responsible, the Ministry or the Competent Authority to adopt any regulations [and establish, as appropriate, 'Welfare Codes', standards and guidance] in this context. The Minister responsible, the Ministry or the Competent Authority shall introduce prescribed minimum standards for animal welfare housing systems. In addition, the Minister responsible, the Ministry or the Competent Authority may require prior authorisation for the manufacture, importation and/or use of any fabricated housing system. The Minister responsible, the Ministry or the Competent Authority shall prohibit ways of keeping animals which are manifestly inconsistent with the principles of animal welfare, including but not limited to the use of certain types of cages and the keeping of animals which are not nocturnal in prevailing darkness.

Section 13 Qualifications of the Animal Keeper

(1) Every person capable of complying with the provisions of the subject Act, and the regulations ['Welfare Codes', standards and guidance] based on it, is authorised to keep animals unless they have been banned from keeping animals due to prior infringements of the subject Act or any other legislation.

(2) Any person who is the keeper of an animal must have the necessary knowledge and required skills and capabilities to safeguard the animal's well-being and provide appropriate and humane management and handling. This would include ensuring appropriate food and nourishment, liquid, care, hygiene, shelter and accommodation, opportunity for exercise and appropriate social interaction – in accordance with the animal's physiological and behavioural needs.

(3) Every keeper of an animal is obliged to ensure that he/she has access to all relevant information, advice and education/training to meet all legislative requirements and provide for all welfare needs of any animal under his/her care.

(4) Every animal owner giving an animal into the care of a keeper is obliged to ensure that the said keeper has the necessary knowledge and required skills and capabilities to safeguard the animal's well-being and provide appropriate and humane management and handling.

(5) Without the consent of their legal guardian minors under the age of 14 years are not allowed to obtain animals.

(6) In addition: Authorisation of the Minister responsible the Ministry or the Competent Authority to adopt any regulations [and establish, as appropriate, 'Welfare Codes', standards and guidance] in this context; including, requirements for the provision of proof of skills, capabilities and knowledge, and detailed provisions governing the keeper's 'duty of care'.

Section 14 Care in Case of Illness or Injury

The owner of an animal who appears to be ill or injured, or in pain or distress, and any keeper of such an animal, must ensure that the animal is inspected, cared for and treated appropriately, and as comprehensively as possible, and without delay. A veterinarian must be consulted whenever the cause of any health issues, illness, injury or other possible emergency cannot be identified. Any ill or injured animal shall be accommodated in consideration of and according to their special needs and if required in separate accommodation. No ill or injured animal shall be transported, unless for emergency purposes and to ensure the animal's welfare.

B. Special Regulations

Section 15   Principles of Animal Breeding

(1) Natural breeding or artificial breeding and reproduction methods, including through methods of bio or gene technology, are prohibited when it is expected that through the breeding or due to the breeding aim either the parent animal, the offspring itself and/or their descendants will be imposed/burdened for a significant period of time or permanently with either pain, suffering or damage or behavioural disorders (including disruption to their species-specific behaviours) or if their physical functions are impaired or disturbed/affected [inhumane breeding practices]. This will particularly be the case where an animal will have any body parts or organs incapacitated/indisposed, altered or missing. It also includes the prohibition of breeding selection for increased aggressiveness or fighting readiness.

(2) Breeding methods and practices which result in, or are likely to result in, birthing difficulties are also considered as 'inhumane breeding practices', and are prohibited.

(3) It is prohibited to pass on, sell, offer for sale, purchase, import or export any animal with features resulting from inhumane breeding practices, or likely to contribute to such inhumane breeding practices.

(4) Breeding should take into account positive animal welfare traits, such as, but not limited to, disease resistance, maternal ability, polled animals etc.

(5) In addition: Authorisation of the Minister responsible, the Ministry or the Competent Authority to adopt any regulations [and establish, as appropriate, 'Welfare Codes', standards and guidance] in the context of breeding and production of animals. This would include: restrictions and prohibitions on certain reproduction methods and breeding aims; restrictions and prohibitions on the breeding or production of certain species or breeds of animal and animals with certain characteristics, and here especially abnormalities in physique/body frame and/or behaviour.

Section 16   Keeping of Animals within the Scope of Business Activities

(1) Keeping (even temporarily) or breeding animals within the scope of business or economic activities falls under the category of activities which require an authorisation in accordance with Section 29. This shall include Commercial Companion Animal Breeders.

This authorisation shall usually be in the form of a license or registration issued by the Competent Authority or their authorised agents.

(2) An application for authorisation must be submitted to the Competent Authority, and be granted before the business or economic activity commences. The application must include, as a minimum,

1.   Details of the type of business/economic activity;
2.   The person responsible for the business/economic activity;
3.   Address and details of the premises/establishment;
4.   Numbers and species of animals kept;
5.   Details of enclosures and dimensions, including photographs;
6.   Details of employees and relevant skills/expertise;
7.   Name of veterinarian(s) and relevant expertise/post-graduate training; and
8.   A full explanation of how the provisions of this Act and, explicitly, the welfare needs of the animals will be met.

(3) The business or economic enterprise shall keep available for inspection by the Competent Authority, at all reasonable times, evidence of the numbers and species/breeds of animals kept/bred; the number and names of employees, and proof of their relevant skills/training; and the care regime instituted to protect the welfare of the animals.

(4) Any person or enterprise keeping or breeding animals within the scope of business or economic activity which changes its location shall immediately notify the Competent Authority of its new premises.

(5) If the Competent Authority has any doubts about the ability of the business or economic enterprise to meet the animal welfare needs of the animals in its operations, it shall deny authorisation, or revoke the same if already granted.

(6) The business or economic activity may not be exercised until authorisation has been granted. The Competent Authority shall prohibit anyone not holding an authorisation from exercising the activity.

(7) The Competent Authority may also close business premises or offices to prevent those which are not covered by an authorisation from the Competent Authority (either because this has not been granted or because authorisation has been revoked) from exercising any business or economic activities keeping or breeding animals. In such cases, every effort must be made to find solutions for the relocation or disposal of any remaining animals which maximise the welfare potential of each individual animal. Careful consideration must also be paid to adopt optimum transitional periods for any prohibitions on certain activities, given the need to secure the welfare of any remaining animals.

(8) Keepers or producers of animals for business or economic activities shall only be permitted to purchase or acquire animals from authorised breeders.

(9) Keepers or producers of animals for business or economic activities bear the responsibility for ensuring that any animals no longer suitable for the business or economic activity in question are rehomed or sent to a shelter or sanctuary wherever possible; or disposed of humanely when no other option exists.

(10) In addition: Authorisation of the Minister responsible, the Ministry or the Competent Authority to adopt any regulations [and establish, as appropriate, 'Welfare Codes', standards and guidance] in this context.

Section 17   Sale and Trading of Animals

(1) Any person, business or economic enterprise selling or transferring the ownership of an animal to another person or enterprise shall provide the person or enterprise taking custody of the animal with relevant information and advice on how to safeguard and protect the animal's welfare, health and well-being. This shall include (as appropriate), but not be restricted to: how to keep, care for, and handle such animal; preventing unwanted breeding; and the vaccinations and other health requirements recommended for the animal offered for sale; as well as any requirements or restrictions on the keeping or breeding of such animals. Evidence of compliance with this obligation must be retained, and made available for inspection by the Competent Authority on request, at all reasonable times.

(2) The trading or sale of animals as a commercial activity requires an authorisation in accordance with Section 29.

(3) An application for authorisation must be submitted to the Competent Authority, and be granted before the trading or selling activity commences. The application must include, as a minimum,

1.   Details of the type of trading or selling activity;
2.   The person responsible for the trading or selling activity;
3.   The species of the animals concerned (and maximum number of animals to be traded or sold);
4.   Address and details of the premises/establishment;

5. Details of employees and relevant skills/expertise; and
6. A full explanation of how the provisions of this Act and, explicitly, the welfare needs of the animals will be met.

(4) Any person or enterprise trading or selling animals shall keep available for inspection by the Competent Authority, at all reasonable times, evidence of the numbers and species of all animals purchased/acquired and sold; the origin and/or destination of the animals; the number and names of employees, and proof of each employee's relevant skills/training; and the care regime instituted to protect the welfare of the animals, including their health status and vaccination history.

(5) Any person or enterprise trading or selling animals who changes its location shall immediately notify the Competent Authority of its new location.

(6) The Competent Authority shall deny authorisation, or revoke the same if already granted, if it has any doubts about the ability of the person or enterprise trading or selling animals to meet the animal's welfare needs in its operations.

(7) The trading or selling enterprise may not be exercised until authorisation has been granted. The Competent Authority shall prohibit anyone not holding an authorisation from exercising the trading or selling activity.

(8) The Competent Authority may also close business premises or offices to prevent those which are not covered by an authorisation from the Competent Authority (either because this has not been granted or because authorisation has been revoked) from exercising any trading or selling activities involving animals.

(9) Traders and sellers of companion animals shall only be permitted to purchase or acquire animals from commercial companion animal breeders who have been duly authorised by the Competent Authority or its designated agents.

(10) Dogs and cats may not be presented or displayed for sale in pet shops or any other premises of enterprises using animals within their scope of their business or economic activities.

(11) The trade or sale of certain wild animals and/or wildlife products can be restricted or banned by the Competent Authority. Also, whenever trade is covered by CITES provisions, guidelines or restrictions, then these shall be applied.

(12) In addition: Authorisation of the Minister responsible, the Ministry or the Competent Authority to adopt any regulations [and establish, as appropriate, 'Welfare Codes', standards and guidance] in this context.

Section 18   Abandoned, Stray or Lost Animals and Confiscated Animals

(1) Abandoned, stray or lost animals as well as animals confiscated or taken away by the responsible authorities, or their designated agents, that cannot be returned to the original rightful owner or keeper have to be transferred by the responsible authorities or their designated agents, to a person, institution or organisation appropriately authorised in accordance with Section 29. These persons, institutions or organisations will be custodians for the animal and thus take over all obligations and responsibilities which normally concern the animal's owner or keeper including all relevant animal welfare requirements according to the subject Act [and any regulations, 'Welfare Codes', standards or guidance under the Act].

(2) For carrying out agreed functions associated with (1) above, the authorised animal shelter, person or institution in question will receive appropriate compensation from the Competent Authorities or their designated agents in form of remuneration to be agreed upon between the two parties. This should cover both compensation for services and repayment of any reasonable expenses incurred relating to these services.

(3) Any person finding an abandoned, stray or lost animal has to inform the relevant authorities *(for instance: the Police, the Competent Authority or their designated agents directly)*, who must arrange for the animal to be collected by or delivered to an appropriately authorised person, institution or organisation according to the subject Act for safeguarding if an owner cannot be located immediately.

(4) The Competent Authority is responsible for ensuring that details of any animal found within its territorial jurisdiction is publicised in a manner widely accessible to the public.

(5) Once a stray or lost animal has been collected and delivered to an authorised person, institution or organisation, it can only be handed over to any persons claiming to be the animal's owner or keeper if there is adequate proof of ownership or custodianship, no liability for abandonment or any breech of animal welfare provisions, and payment has been made for any service charges and expenses incurred. The owner is prohibited from requiring the animal to be euthanised to avoid such costs but instead has the option to transfer ownership to the authorised person, institution or organisation for rehoming.

(6) If there is no substantiated request for handing over made by an animal's owner or keeper(s) within one month from the date of publication, according to paragraph (4) above, then ownership of the animal may be transferred to new owners, who, after investigation, appear to be capable of taking care of the welfare of the animal.

(7) In addition: Authorisation of the Minister responsible, the Ministry or the Competent Authority to adopt any regulations [and establish, as appropriate, 'Welfare Codes', standards and guidance] in this context. In any cases where straying is found to be problematic for the authorities or the public, then compulsory identification and registration should be introduced.

Section 19   General and Commercial Transport of Animals

(1) The transport of an animal, which includes any kind of transfer or relocation of the animal from one place to another as well as the loading and unloading of the animal, has to be undertaken in a careful and considerate way at all times. Also, the length of any journey, and of any delay at any stage of transport, shall be minimised.

(2) Each animal must be provided with sufficient food, water and rest before, during and after the journey, according to their biological and ethological needs.

(3) The method of transport shall be suitable with regard to the welfare and safety of the animal, and the animal's species-specific and individual character.

(4) It is prohibited to transport an animal in a way that causes pain, injury, death or avoidable suffering, fear or distress to the animal.

(5) It is in particular prohibited to transport

1.   A late pregnant female;
2.   A female during one week after giving birth;
3.   New-born animals – for example, when the navel has not completely healed; or
4.   An animal who is ill, injured, weak, or in general unfit for the journey;

unless the journey is in the welfare interests of the individual animal.

(6) When transporting an animal for commercial purposes, the following additional requirements and conditions have to be observed:

1.   The animal must be healthy and fit for the journey, and certified as such by an official veterinarian appointed by the Competent Authority.
2.   The animal shall have the necessary supervision and care during transportation and loading/unloading.

3. The means of transport as well as the loading and unloading facilities, procedures and equipment have to be designed, constructed, maintained and operated in a way that the safety and well-being of the animal is guaranteed at any given time, and any pain, injury, suffering, fear or distress avoided.

4. The animal has to be provided with adequate floor area, space and height as well as with sufficient ventilation and protection against unfavourable weather conditions.

5. An animal shall only be transported in a vehicle or container that has been inspected and certified by the Competent Authority.

6. In case of the transport of aquatic animals, this must be carried out in special means of transportation and/or specially-designed containers; and the amount of water available must be sufficient for the number of animals transported, as well as of appropriate quality and temperature, and a satisfactory supply of oxygen ensured.

7. In the case that the upright position of the container transporting an animal is not evident, the container in question has to bear a sign or marking indicating the said position.

8. In case it is not obvious from the nature or style of the container that it transports a live animal, the container has to be clearly labelled indicating the fact that it contains an animal, and at the same time identifying the animal species within.

9. During transport the condition of the animal has to be checked at regular intervals and concurrently it has to be ensured that the animal has sufficient water and food of appropriate quality and suitability for the animal's species-specific and individual needs. There shall be both specific official 'staging posts' (authorised in accordance with Section 29) with official supervision and control, and also random unannounced checks.

10. Any business which transports animals must be registered and authorised by the Competent Authority in accordance with Section 29. Authorisation may be withdrawn in the event of breaches of this code, or temporarily suspended until infringements have been rectified.

11. The persons driving vehicles transporting live animals or handling animals during the transport process must have the necessary professional, technical and personal skills, and understanding of animal behaviour, to care for the welfare needs of the animals in their care.

12. Drivers of livestock vehicles should be trained in necessary driving techniques, and always take extreme care to avoid acceleration, deceleration or turning corners at excessive speed. They should have their licences endorsed with the species of animals they have been trained and certified to transport.

13. No animal shall be transported commercially without prior approval from the Competent Authority. The Competent Authority shall provide detailed regulations governing live animal transport authorisation procedures. These shall include: the advance submission of route plans (together with required contents and submission periods for advance notifications); and the issue of movement permits based on company registration and driver/handler certification; and veterinary checks of fitness, vehicle compliance, and compliance with feeding/watering/resting requirements.

14. Journey plans and preparations must include the provision of veterinary attention to deal with any ill or injured animals; and disease control and emergency response measures.

15. During transportation of an animal, the transporter shall, at all times, carry the permit issued by the Competent Authority and other documents relevant for animal movement issued under this Act. A person shall not transport an animal in any manner other than that certified in the permit.

16. The Competent Authority shall lay down rules and regulations on establishing the fitness of an animal for transport, maximum journey times, set regular rest intervals as well as feeding and watering times. Every effort should be made to reduce the long distance transport of live animals, particularly for killing/slaughter (with animals being slaughtered locally, and carcasses transported instead of live animals).

17. International trade, long distance transport and transportation by sea or air shall only be carried out under special licenses/permits from the Competent Authority. Such licenses/permits shall contain additional conditions/requirements, as well as taking necessary measures to protect individual species. Such transport shall be prohibited for species with particular welfare problems during above mentioned transport.

(7) Both the transporter and the owner of the animal (if different) shall be responsible for ensuring compliance with these provisions

(8) In addition: Authorisation of the Minister responsible, the Ministry or the Competent Authority to adopt any regulations [and establish, as appropriate, 'Welfare Codes', standards and guidance] in this context.

Section 20   Humane Killing and Slaughter of Animals

(1) Without prejudice to the prohibition of killing animals according to Section 9 and notwithstanding Section 7, the killing of an animal has at all times to be carried out in compliance with the subject Act as well as in a humane way and in such a manner that the animal is spared any avoidable pain, suffering, injury, fear or distress.

(2) Without prejudice to the prohibition of killing animals according to Section 9 and notwithstanding Section 7, the deliberate killing of vertebrates is only allowed to be performed by veterinarians or trained and registered, certified, or licensed veterinary assistants under the supervision of a veterinarian. This is not applicable to

1.   Professionally skilled killing of farmed or game animals;
2.   Emergency killing; or
3.   Professional 'pest' control work.

(3) It is prohibited to kill or slaughter any animal without prior and effective anaesthetisation or stunning before death supervenes without the recovery of consciousness (for example, through exsanguination in commercial slaughter); unless animals are killed instantaneously. In cases where stunning or anaesthetisation do not produce immediate unconsciousness, the induction of unconsciousness must be completely non-aversive, and not cause any pain, suffering, injury, fear or distress. When stunning is used to induce unconsciousness before slaughter, the time between stunning and exsanguinations must be kept as short as possible to prevent animals recovering from the stunning before exsanguination.

(4) If in the case of an emergency killing it is not possible to render prior effective anaesthetisation or stunning to the animal, killing or slaughter shall be performed in such a manner that minimises any pain, suffering, injury, fear or distress.

(5) An animal's life shall not be terminated

1.   By drowning or any other method of suffocation;
2.   By using any poisonous substance or drug, except when administered by a veterinarian or a certified, licensed or registered veterinary assistant under the supervision of a veterinarian;
3.   Using any percussion instrument which does not produce the effect required in sub-section (1) and (3); or
4.   By electrocution, unless preceded by immediate induction of loss of consciousness.

(6) In all cases, the person responsible for terminating the animal's life shall ensure that the animal is dead before the carcass is manipulated, disposed of or used in any way (such as butchering or skinning).

(7) Only persons who have the necessary professional, technical and personal knowledge and skills (and have received appropriate training) shall perform tasks connected to the killing/slaughter process: animal unloading and movement; accommodation and care of the animal in the lairage and slaughterhouse; and the restraint, stunning and anaesthetisation as well as the humane killing, slaughtering and exsanguination of the animal. The Competent Authority shall establish a system of certification to enable personnel to demonstrate compliance with these requirements.

(8) All slaughterhouses and their installations, equipment and instruments must be designed, constructed, maintained and operated in a way that the well-being of the animal is safeguarded and any pain, injury, suffering, fear or distress avoided as far as possible. All businesses operating and managing slaughterhouses shall be

authorised in accordance with Section 29.

(9) No installations, equipment, instruments and substances/preparations for the stunning, killing or restraint of animals shall be used commercially without first obtaining a licence from the Competent Authority according to Section 29.

(10) The Competent Authority may wish to add a provision here to set out any desired restrictions or conditions concerning home killing/slaughter for personal consumption. If this is the case, then the need to comply with general conditions for humane killing/slaughter need to be stipulated, including the requirement to spare the animal avoidable pain, distress or suffering during the process.

(11) Ritual/religious slaughter: The Competent Authority may decide to completely prohibit ritual/religious slaughter, or to restrict this significantly – only allowing this in especially established and authorised slaughterhouses and solely designated for the consumption of the relevant religious community. Here, consideration could be given to specifying which religious grouping should be entitled to these exemptions, and explicitly limiting quantities according to the size of the individual community. In any case where ritual/religious slaughter is permitted, then it should be well controlled, and clear labelling made compulsory. If permitted on this basis, then the Competent Authority would need to establish further detailed conditions and requirements.
If a decision is taken to prohibit ritual/religious slaughter, then relevant constitutional provisions (for example, regarding religious freedoms) would need to be examined, and consideration given as to whether a constitutional amendment is necessary to accommodate this approach.

12) In addition: Authorisation of the Minister responsible, the Ministry or the Competent Authority to adopt any regulations [and establish, as appropriate, 'Welfare Codes', standards and guidance] in this context.

Section 21   Principles of Animal Training

(1) Notwithstanding Section 7, the training of any animal for sports, performance, or exhibition has to be accomplished in compliance with the subject Act, as well as in a humane way, using only positive reinforcement and natural behavioural traits as opposed to negative reinforcement or punishment, and in such a manner that the animal is spared any avoidable pain, suffering, injury, fear or distress.

(2) No person or business shall exhibit or train any animal for commercial competitive or public sports, performances or exhibitions; unless he/she is registered and authorised in accordance with Section 29.

(3) The Competent Authority shall prohibit [or restrict] the training of certain species of animals or the training of animals for certain types of sports, performances or exhibition, if this could impair the welfare of the animals.

(4) The Competent Authority shall prohibit [or restrict] the use of any substances or drugs to enhance an animal's performance or modify its behaviour or temperament for sports, performance or exhibition purposes.

(5) The Competent Authority shall prohibit [or restrict] the use of certain technical training devices, aids or tools which could impair the welfare of animals trained for sports, performance or exhibition.

(6) A person shall not use a live animal as lure or bait to train a dog or any other animal, or to test his or her aggressiveness.

(7) The Competent Authority shall carry out unannounced inspection visits to ensure that any animal training complies with the requirements of this Act and any regulations [and, as appropriate, 'Welfare Codes', standards and guidance] made under it.

(8) In addition: Authorisation of the Minister responsible, the Ministry or the Competent Authority to adopt any regulations [and establish, as appropriate, 'Welfare Codes', standards and guidance] in this context.

CHAPTER 4: SPECIFIC CATEGORIES OF ANIMAL USE

Section 22　Companion Animals (Pet Animals)

(1) The Competent Authority shall support education and awareness of responsible companion animal ownership, including within schools.

(2) Where there is a problem with stray management, over-population, or concerns connected with animal welfare, rabies or other health/safety problems; there shall be compulsory registration and identification of dogs, cats or any other species of companion animal involved. Where compulsory registration is introduced, the Competent Authority shall establish a public database to record registration information.

(3) The Competent Authority shall introduce compulsory vaccination against any prevalent preventative zoonotic diseases, including rabies.

(4) The Competent Authority shall implement or support services to reduce stray populations, including free or low cost spay-neuter services for feral cats and dogs, and dogs and cats owned by disadvantaged people or kept as community animals.

(5) Any owned dogs, cats, and other animals which are allowed to roam freely shall be spay-neutered, at the owner's expense if no governmental or other free spay-neuter services are available, to prevent further over-population.

(6) Whenever population control measures are to be undertaken, the most humane and effective methods shall be used at all stages of the process. The Competent Authority shall support and encourage the use of Trap, Neuter and Release (TNR) programmes for feral and wild animals where population control measures are considered necessary and this is deemed to be in the welfare interests of the animals. In such cases neutering must be carried out by a trained veterinarian, and the animals returned to their original habitat after recovery.

(7) In accordance with Section 9 (Prohibition of Killing Animals) it is prohibited to kill a healthy stray companion animal which has the opportunity of being placed in a home or taken by an animal shelter or sanctuary authorised in accordance with Section 29 or to a pound; or, in the case of feral cats and feral dogs, they can be neutered and returned to their habitat.

(8) Animal shelters and pounds have a duty to try to rehome all healthy, animals suitable for adoption, through advertising and awareness, and making these readily available for adoption. Animals must be kept for a reasonable time period for reclaiming or adoption. Public pounds shall be open to members of the public for reclaim or adoption seven days per week.

(9) The Minister responsible, the Ministry or the Competent Authority shall create a list of species which are allowed to be kept as companion animals, based on clear criteria including animal welfare (and other relevant concerns).

(10) In addition: Authorisation of the Minister responsible, the Ministry or the Competent Authority to adopt any regulations [and establish, as appropriate, 'Welfare Codes', standards and guidance] in this context.

Section 23   Animals Kept for Farming Purposes

(1) The Competent Authority shall prescribe minimum standards for housing systems for farmed animals, including bird housing and fish farming systems, to ensure that these meet the animal welfare requirements of this Act including, but not limited to, Section 12.

(2) A person shall not manufacture, keep in stock, sell, offer for sale, deliver, or in any manner make use of an animal housing system unless such a system is built, maintained and conforms to the prescribed minimum standards for animal welfare.

(3) The Competent Authority shall establish a scheme of prior approval for commercial animal housing systems and installations in accordance with Section 29. Such prior approval shall be based on application from the manufacturer, importer or retailer of these systems and installations; which shall be accompanied by a report stating how the system meets animal welfare requirements. All modern intensive farming systems shall incorporate a CCTV system to ensure effective monitoring and inspection.

(4) The Competent Authority may revoke a permit issued to a manufacturer, importer or retailer where

1.   The information submitted at the time of the application was incorrect or misleading in such a manner that, had the information been known at the time the permit was granted, the application would have been rejected; or
2.   In the opinion of the Competent Authority, circumstances exist which are detrimental to the welfare or safety of any animal.

(5) The Competent Authority may restrict the manufacture, importation, supply, sale or use of any housing system or installation which does not conform to the required animal welfare standards.

(6) The owner and keeper shall ensure that the condition and state of the health of an animal kept for farming purposes shall be thoroughly inspected at intervals sufficient to avoid unnecessary suffering; this shall be at least once a day, and more frequently in the case of animals kept in modern intensive farming systems and/or housing systems.

(7) The technical equipment used in modern intensive farming systems and/or housing systems shall be thoroughly inspected at least once a day; and any defect discovered shall be remedied with the least possible delay. When a defect cannot be remedied forthwith, all temporary measures necessary to safeguard the welfare of the animals shall be taken immediately.

(8) The Competent Authority shall inspect each farm at least once each year, to ensure continued compliance with this Act and any regulations [and 'Welfare Codes', standards and guidance] made under it.

(9) The Minister responsible, the Ministry or the Competent Authority shall adopt regulations to prohibit ways of keeping farmed animals, including birds and fish, which are manifestly inconsistent with the principles of animal welfare including, but not limited to, the use of certain types of cages and systems which are known to cause inherent animal welfare problems, such as: veal crates for calves; sow stalls (also known as gestation crates) and tethers for pregnant pigs; farrowing crates for sows; battery cages for egg laying hens; and the permanent confinement of dairy cows.

(10) The Minister responsible, the Ministry or the Competent Authority shall adopt regulations to prohibit the keeping of farmed animals, including birds and fish, for inessential, luxury products; particularly where their production incurs animal welfare problems, restricts their species-specific or behavioural needs, or affects their intrinsic value.

(11) The Minister responsible, the Ministry or the Competent Authority shall issue regulations to prohibit farming practices which are manifestly inconsistent with the principles of animal welfare, including: the keeping of animals in darkness; forced molting; plucking of down from live ducks and geese; force feeding of ducks and geese for 'foie gras'; and feeding calves with insufficient quantities of fibrous food to maintain them in good health and welfare.

(12) The Minister responsible, the Ministry or the Competent Authority shall create a list of species which are allowed to be kept for farming purposes, based on clear criteria including animal welfare. No new species shall be added to the list unless the Competent Authority is satisfied that there is a case of need; the requirements of this Act can be met at all stages of their life-cycle; and the animals' welfare can be maintained and provided for in a manner which meets all their species-specific and individual needs.

(13) In addition: Authorisation of the Minister responsible, the Ministry or the Competent Authority to adopt any regulations [and establish, as appropriate, 'Welfare Codes', standards and guidance] in this context.

Section 24   Animals Used for Experimentation (including Science, Research, Testing and Education)

(1) No person shall conduct any experiment on an animal without prior authorisation from the Competent Authority in the form of a personal license in accordance with Section 29. A personal license may only be granted where the applicant has the appropriate qualifications, training, experience and character.

(2) No person shall conduct any experiment on an animal without prior authorisation for the project in question from the Competent Authority, in the form of a project license, in accordance with Section 29. This authorisation shall take into account the opinion issued by the Animal Experimentation Sub-Committee referred to in Article 35 (4) of this Act. Such authorisation shall specify the practice for which it has been granted; the species and number of animals involved; the named person responsible for the experiment and the welfare of the animals; details of veterinary supervision; the period of validity of the authorisation; and any restrictions and conditions which the Competent Authority may determine.

(3) An application to carry out an animal experiment must be accompanied by an explanation as to ethical and scientific justification to conduct the experiment; and a full explanation of how the Three Rs have been taken into account in its design and planning.

(4) The Competent Authority shall only grant the authorisation referred to in Section 24 (2) for experiments that are intended to benefit the health or welfare of humans or animals or the protection of the environment; providing these also meet the following requirements:

1. There is a clear ethical and scientific justification for the experiment.
2. There is clear evidence that the Three Rs have been fully taken into account in the experiment's design and planning.
3. The experiment in question, and the associated keeping and care of the animals, comply with the provisions of this Act in all respects.
4. Such experiment complies with all subsequent regulations, ethical rules and standards prescribed by the Competent Authority.

(5) The internationally-recognised 'Three Rs' shall be stringently applied to the care and use of live animals for experimentation. These are

1. Replacement of animals with non-animal techniques,
2. Reduction in numbers of animals, and
3. Refinement of experimental methods.

Prime consideration should always be given to the avoidance of any methods using live animals: This means not carrying out any experiments using live animals whenever this could be avoided – by abandoning any non-essential experiments and/or using alternative non-animal methods. A non-animal method is considered to be valid for use if it has been approved. The government will consider on a case by case basis whether an alternative method is acceptable, and where there are standard methods, regularly update the list of animal tests that are no longer permitted due to the availability of alternative methods. Where replacement with an alternative method is not deemed possible, then the numbers of animals used should be reduced as far as possible (for example, by implementing testing strategies, such as the use of in vitro and other methods); and refining the methods, procedures and systems used, and care given to the maximum extent in order to minimise impact on animal welfare.

(6) It is explicitly prohibited to use animals in experiments for the following purposes:

1. The testing of weapons, ammunition or associated equipment, war equipment and the effects of radiation;
2. The research or development of tobacco products;
3. The research or development of alcoholic products and narcotics or other recreational drugs; or
4. The research or development of cosmetic products and household products (including chemical cleaning and disinfection products) or ingredients or combinations of ingredients primarily intended for these purposes.

The Competent Authority may add to this list of prohibited uses at any time, through the use of specific regulations.

(7) It shall be prohibited to carry out any experiment on a non-human primate or a cetacean which is not in the animal's welfare interests or has the potential of affecting the animal's longevity.

The Competent Authority may add to this list of species prohibited for the purposes of animal experimentation at any time, through the use of specific regulations.

(8) It shall be prohibited to import, export, sell or offer for sale, any products which have been developed or tested using animal experimentation since the date when the use of animals for the said purpose was explicitly prohibited.

(9) A person shall not conduct an experiment on any animal which has not been purpose-bred in a breeding centre licensed by the Competent Authority in accordance with Section 29.

(10) Animal experiments shall only be conducted in premises that have been specifically licensed for this purpose by the Competent Authority in accordance with Section 29.

(11) No person shall work with animals in experimentation unless they have the qualifications, training and competence to satisfy the requirements of this Act and any subsequent regulations, ethical rules and standards prescribed by the Competent Authority.

(12) It shall be the duty of the named person responsible for the experiment to ensure that the experiment on an animal is conducted in accordance with the authorisation provided by the Competent Authority and the provisions of this Act and any subsequent regulations, ethical rules and standards prescribed by the Competent Authority. Every experiment shall have veterinary supervision to ensure the welfare of the animal.

(13) The named person responsible for the experiment shall ensure that, where the animal on which the experiment is being carried out could experience pain, injury, fear or distress as a result of acts carried out without anaesthesia, a general or local anaesthetic is administered to the animal to prevent these adverse states impacting its welfare.

(14) The named person responsible for the experiment shall also ensure that an animal which, if allowed to live, would suffer pain or distress for a prolonged period as a result of an act performed as part of the experiment, is

immediately put to death humanely. In no case should any animal be used for more than one experiment unless this is benign research which has not impaired the animal's welfare in any way.

(15) Detailed records must be kept of the animals bred, sold and acquired for experiments; the number of experiments and procedures carried out on animals and the animals discarded and not subsequently used; including species and numbers of animals involved in each category. These records shall be submitted to the Competent Authority at least once a year in the format required by the Competent Authority.

(16) The results of all animal experiments shall be made available to the Competent Authority to enable them to assess any duplication. The Competent Authority has the authority to make any results available to the public, if this is in the public interests: This includes the need to avoid duplication of animal experimentation and the development of inessential or unnecessary experiments. The Competent Authority shall publish electronically an annual overview of experiments licensed, including the numbers, species and broad areas of use.

(17) The Competent Authority shall inspect each licensed breeding facility and licensed premises where animal experiments are carried out at least once per year. Such inspections shall be aimed at ensuring compliance with the requirements of this Act and any subsequent regulations, ethical rules and standards prescribed by the Competent Authority, and include: physical checks on the premises, facilities and equipment; systems and procedures; the welfare of the animals used in experimentation (including care and housing); and record inspections.

(18) Animals shall not be used for teaching or educational purposes unless their welfare can be protected at all times; the use is considered essential; and alternatives that do not require the use of animals are not available.

(19) In addition: Authorisation of the Minister responsible, the Ministry or the Competent Authority to adopt any regulations [and establish, as appropriate, 'Welfare Codes', standards and guidance] in this context.

Section 25   Wildlife and Animals Kept in Zoos/Aquaria

(1) The government and all citizens shall make every effort to prevent and avoid detrimental impacts on the welfare of wild animals at large in nature, or in protected areas (such as national parks, wildlife and marine reserves, and conservation areas) by human activities, development and land use.

(2) The Competent Authority shall introduce and use a system of animal welfare impact assessment as a basis for the identification and evaluation of potential detrimental impacts. It is granted the power to introduce any prohibitions, conditions and requirements deemed necessary to prevent such detrimental impacts.

(3) It is prohibited to harm, harass, wound, mutilate, take or kill any wild animal at large in nature, or in protected areas (such as national parks, wildlife and marine reserves, and conservation areas), unless there is a genuine, ascertainable risk to human/animal health or welfare, which can reasonably be shown to outweigh the interests of the wild animal, and the method used causes the least possible pain, suffering, injury, fear or distress.

(4) Where there is overpopulation of wild animals in nature or protected areas, which could lead to starvation, suffering, fear or distress, every effort should be made to carry out humane population management measures, avoiding unnecessary deaths or welfare impacts. Where all possible alternatives have been fully explored and exhausted, and the conclusion is that there is no alternative but to carry out culling, this should be carried out by a professional hunter in such as manner as to prevent suffering, in accordance with the provisions of this Act. No animal culled as part of a conservation process can be used for commercial purposes. All population management measures should take account of the need to avoid disruption to social hierarchies and/or family groupings.

(5) In order to protect indigenous wildlife and their habitats, the Competent Authority shall strictly control the introduction of non-native species. Only indigenous wildlife shall be kept in nature and protected areas.

(6) It is prohibited to take, remove, destroy, harm or disturb any nests, eggs or breeding sites in the wild.

(7) The Competent Authority shall establish a positive list of wild animal species which are permitted to be kept by private individuals and organisations. This list shall only include species for which the requirements of this Act can be met at all stages of their life-cycle. It shall be regularly reviewed in order to take into account any relevant advances in animal welfare science and/or any emergent welfare problems.

(8) Any hunting or killing of captive wildlife on private property shall only be permitted if prior authorisation has been granted by the Competent Authority, in the form of a hunting license specifying the property in question and the species to be hunted in accordance with Section 29. Each hunting premise shall keep full records of all wild animals; including species kept, number, and their origin and disposal.

(9) The only persons who shall be permitted to hunt on licensed hunting premises shall be individuals who have received a hunting proficiency certificate issued by the Competent Authority and professional hunters who have an advanced proficiency certificate issued by the Competent Authority. In all cases, hunting must be by, or under the supervision of, a professional hunter. The professional hunter shall be responsible for ensuring that animal welfare requirements and the provisions of this Act are met. Any person, who has been convicted for violating any animal protection provision, or for any act of violence or aggression against humans, shall be considered ineligible for a hunting proficiency certificate.

(10) Hunting with dogs, from horseback, or from vehicles or aircraft is prohibited.

(11) Hunting must always use humane killing methods, which meet the criteria set out in Section 20.

(12) The capture, restraint, entanglement, immobilisation or killing of wild animals by inhumane methods including, but not limited to, snares, leg-hold traps, glue-boards or other adhesive traps, anti-coagulant poisons, bows, crossbows, and explosives other than firearms ammunition is prohibited. The use of methods deemed inhumane and not recommended for authorisation by the Animal Welfare Committee are likewise prohibited; as is the sale, offering for sale, advertising, import and export of such unauthorised catching, trapping or killing devices, including poisons.

(13) Any wild animals injured but not killed during hunting or culling must be immediately found and humanely killed.

(14) The capture, chasing or killing of wild animals for entertainment is prohibited.

(15) The hunting or killing of wild animals for inessential purposes such as trophies; decorations; cosmetic and vanity products; and medicinal products and potions which do not have proven beneficial health effects shall not be permitted. The sale, offer for sale, import or export of such wild animal trophies; decorations; cosmetic and vanity products; medicinal products and potions shall be prohibited.

(16) Where wild animals come into the human domain and are considered to be causing considerable danger, health hazard or nuisance, then every effort should be made to ensure that any deterrent or population management measures are carried out humanely, avoiding unnecessary deaths or adverse welfare impacts. Wherever possible, humane preventative measures must be taken as opposed to remedial action. Where all possible alternatives have been fully explored and exhausted, and the conclusion is that there is no alternative left but to capture, entrap or kill such animals, and there is any reason to believe that if this is not carried out professionally there may be a danger of a breach of the provisions of this subject Act or any regulations made under it, this should only be carried out by a veterinarian, a licensed animal control/'pest' control professional or a professional hunter (as appropriate) - who has been trained and certified in humane control methods and authorised in accordance with Section 29 for the species in question. Only methods of capture, entrapment or killing authorised by the Competent Authority, on the advice of the Animal Welfare Committee which has deemed these to be humane and in accordance with the provisions of this Act, shall be used for this purpose.

(17) Wild animals should not be kept in captivity unless there is an ethical justification for their captivity based on

a proven and overriding benefit to human or animal life, conservation or welfare; the requirements of this Act can be met at all stages of their life-cycle; and the animal's welfare can be maintained and provided for in a manner which meets all their species-specific and individual needs; including an environment as close to their natural habitat as possible (which permits the performance of natural behaviours), and the provision of specialist veterinary expertise.

(18) In cases where such use is permitted by the Competent Authority in accordance with Section 29, the authorisation process in Section 16 shall be followed, and the Competent Authority shall closely monitor compliance with this Act, with a view to prohibiting categories of use or individual authorisations in all cases where compliance cannot be ensured.

(19) Zoological gardens (Zoos and Aquaria) shall only be authorised (as per Section 16 and in accordance with Section 29) if they have been accredited by the World Association of Zoos and Aquaria (WAZA), and they can demonstrate that they are carrying out valuable conservation programmes aimed at breeding and reintroducing endangered wild animals back into sustainable wildlife habitats; and are carrying out effective conservation and animal welfare work, including benign wildlife welfare research.

20) The Competent Authority may authorise the temporary keeping of wild animals for the purpose of providing an injured, damaged or otherwise impaired wild animal with the proper medical and veterinary treatment and necessary care for a recovery to full health in a wildlife rehabilitation centre authorised in accordance with Section 38 before its release back into free nature (or keeping in an authorised animal sanctuary if such release is not possible or in the animal's welfare interests, given its current physical or psychological condition).

(21) It shall be a requirement of the authorisation for keeping wild animals to keep accurate and up-to-date records of all wild animals held, including species, numbers, births, deaths, acquisitions (and origins) and disposals (and destinations). There shall also be a written programme of veterinary care prescribed by a veterinarian with experience of caring for the species. This data shall be submitted to the Competent Authority in an annual return, and they shall ensure that details are entered onto a centralised system to secure traceability and effective enforcement. The Competent Authority shall check each premise keeping wild animals at least once each year, to ascertain compliance with this Act and that measures are in place to prevent any risks to animal welfare and public health; including necessary veterinary checks. Any movements of wild animals shall be notified to the Competent Authority, and no movements shall take place to persons or premises not authorised to keep wild animals.

(22) It is prohibited to keep or breed wild animals for obtaining furs or other inessential luxury products.

(23) In addition: Authorisation of the Minister responsible, the Ministry or the Competent Authority to adopt any regulations [and establish, as appropriate, 'Welfare Codes', standards and guidance] in this context.

Section 26   Animals Used for Work

(1) Only animals of appropriate breeds or species which are able to carry out the designated work without detrimentally affecting their welfare, shall be used for work. No non-domesticated animal shall be kept for work purposes.

(2) An animal shall not be worked when in poor health, or too young or old to be worked without welfare implications. In all such cases, the animal shall be cared for humanely, and in accordance with the requirements of this Act.

(3) There shall be reasonable limitations on the intensity and duration of the work to be performed by a working animal; including appropriate periods of rest and relaxation. No working animal shall be over-worked, over-loaded, over-driven or made to perform any work that stretches their natural capacities.

(4) Animals used for work shall be provided with adequate shade and shelter, a soft lying area which is free from

any dangerous objects, and adequate space for relaxation during rest periods. In warm climates, effective measures shall be taken to prevent heat stress in animals used for work.

(5) The equipment and fixtures for animals used for work shall be designed to ease carrying capacity and movement, and prevent any bodily damage, injury, harm or strain. No equipment, harnesses, carts, tethers, saddlery, shoes etc. shall be used that compromise the welfare of animals used for work.

(6) Every possible preventative measure shall be taken to avoid road accidents and traffic hold-ups involving animals used for work. Animal carts and vehicles and burden carrying animals used on roads shall be made well visible; and not used in conditions of darkness without appropriate lighting.

(7) Dogs used for work must be under effective control of the human handler at all times, and muzzled where there is any risk of aggression.

(8) Both the owner and the handler (if different) of any animal used for work shall be responsible for ensuring compliance with these provisions.

(9) In addition: Authorisation of the Minister responsible, the Ministry or the Competent Authority to adopt any regulations [and establish, as appropriate, 'Welfare Codes', standards and guidance] in this context.

Section 27   Animals Used for Sports, Leisure and Entertainment

(1) Animals shall only be kept for sports, leisure and entertainment in cases where all the requirements of this Act can be met at all stages of their life-cycle; and the animal's welfare can be maintained and provided for in a manner which meets all their species-specific and individual needs, including the provision of specialist veterinary expertise.

(2) In cases of commercial use of animals for sports, leisure or entertainment, where such use is permitted by the Competent Authority, the authorisation process in Section 16 shall be followed, in accordance with Section 29, and the Competent Authority shall closely monitor compliance with 21 (1) above, with a view to prohibiting categories of use or individual authorisations in all cases where compliance cannot be ensured.

(3) Keeping any species of wild animal for the purposes of sports, leisure and entertainment is prohibited: This prohibition will include circuses, dolphinaria and variety shows (whether itinerant or stationary).

(4) The organising, promotion or advertising of any sport, leisure or entertainment using wild animals is prohibited.

(5) A person shall not organise any sport or event that tests the speed, strength or endurance of an animal unless such sport or event is held in accordance with regulations made under this Act.

(6) A person shall not promote, arrange, participate in, attend, assist at, receive money for or in any way facilitate any event involving the harassing, harming or tormenting of any animal.

(7) Bullfights and rodeos shall be prohibited.

(8) Animals shall not be used for film, still photographs, video or television productions unless their health and welfare can be assured, in training, during production and post-production.

(9) Both the owner and the handler (if different) of any animal used for the purposes of sports, leisure or entertainment shall be responsible for ensuring compliance with these provisions.

(10) The Competent Authority shall regularly re-evaluate the use of animals for the purposes of sports, leisure or entertainment, with a view to prohibiting any uses which can no longer be justified or have been seen to, or are

likely to, impair animal welfare (at any stage of the process – including breeding, training, keeping, transport and killing or disposal).

(11) In addition: Authorisation of the Minister responsible, the Ministry or the Competent Authority to adopt any regulations [and establish, as appropriate, 'Welfare Codes', standards and guidance] in this context.

CHAPTER 5: IMPLEMENTATION AND ENFORCEMENT PROVISIONS

Section 28   Authorities

(1) The Competent Authority responsible for the central animal welfare policy and administrative implementation and enforcement of this Act and any regulations [and 'Welfare Codes', standards and guidance] made under it shall be *[Complete as appropriate. For instance: the Minister or Ministry of Agriculture, Fisheries and Food; of Environment; of Health; of Interior or of Justice]*.

(2) The Competent Authority has to ensure that any secondary legislation [and 'Welfare Codes', standards and guidance] is drafted consistently with the Act, and shall also be responsible for issuing implementation and enforcement instructions and guidance. It may authorise the Veterinary Services to draft or co-ordinate regulations [and establish, as appropriate, 'Welfare Codes', standards and guidance] and/or instructions and guidance of a technical nature. It shall also provide advice and guidance on animal welfare matters.

(3) The implementation and enforcement of compliance with the provisions of this Act and any regulations [and, as appropriate, 'Welfare Codes', standards and guidance] made under it shall be the responsibility of all government officials whose work covers animal issues and/or education and awareness (including but not limited to: veterinary and zoo-sanitary inspectors, veterinary and agricultural extension officers, nature conservation officers/wildlife officers, educators, government communication officers, traffic officers, customs officials and municipal stray management authorities).

(4) The organs of the public security/police shall by virtue of their office be deemed to be enforcement officers/Animal Welfare Inspectors for the general purpose of this Act.

(5) All [regional governments] and local authorities shall also have a duty to enforce this Act and any regulations [and, as appropriate, 'Welfare Codes', standards and guidance] made under it.

(6) A local government authority may make by-laws for the effective implementation and enforcement of this Act in its area of jurisdiction.

(7) The Competent Authority may also appoint as Animal Welfare Inspectors, proficient and experienced animal welfare professionals, including: employees of animal welfare organisations, registered veterinarians and para-professionals. Such appointed Animal Welfare Inspectors shall be given the specified law enforcement powers needed to fulfill their mandate.

(8) Only appropriately trained and experienced professionals shall be licensed as Animal Welfare Inspectors by the Competent Authority or its duly authorised agents.

(9) All enforcement and inspection of the present Act shall be carried out under the supervision of the Competent

Authority, which shall also bear responsibility for ensuring that regular inspections are carried out on all authorised/licensed/registered concerns using animals.

Section 29   Authorisations

(1) Authorisation is required for certain activities involving sentient animals. These would include, but not be restricted to, the following:

1. Keeping or breeding animals within the scope of business or economic activities (as per Section 16), including any species or use as well as animals for commercial sale and animal boarding (e.g. kennelling or livery);
2. Operating a riding or carriage business (as per Section 16 and Section 26);
3. Live animal traction or haulage businesses (as per Section 16 and Section 26);
4. Trading, dealing or sale of animals as a commercial activity (as per Section 17), including: live animal importers or exporters; live animal markets, traders or auctions; 'pet' shops/companion animal sellers;
5. Receiving abandoned, stray or lost, or confiscated animals (as per Section 18);
6. Commercial transport of live animals (as per Section 19);
7. Live animal assembly centres or staging posts (as per Section 19);
8. Operating and managing a slaughterhouse, or any other establishment killing animals for a business or economic activity (as per Section 20);
9. Training any animal for performance, sports or exhibition, including dog training facilities (as per Section 21);
10. Operating an animal shelter, animal sanctuary or wildlife rehabilitation centre (as per Sections 18, 22 and 38);
11. A positive list of the species of animals which may be kept as companion animals (as per Section 22);
12. Commercial animal housing (as per Section 23);
13. Animal experimentation or research (personal licences, project licenses, premises licenses and breeding establishment licenses) (as per Section 24);
14. Hunting (property/species and hunters) (as per Section 25);
15. Animal control businesses (including 'pest control') (as per Section 25);
16. Zoological gardens (Zoos and Aquaria), where permitted for conservation purposes (as per Section 25);
17. Any other keeping of wild animals (as per Section 25);
18. A positive list of wild animal species which are permitted to be kept by private individuals and organisations (as per Section 25);
19. Facilities or businesses using animals for entertainment, leisure, sports or exhibition, including circuses and variety shows *(if permitted)* (as per Section 27); and
20. The use of animals for film, still photographs, video or television productions (as per Section 27).

This authorisation shall usually be in the form of a license issued by the Competent Authority or their authorised agents. This shall specify not only the activity, but also the species of animals covered.
Whereby this list is just a suggestion and shall not be seen as exclusive.

(2) More detailed provisions on the minimum requirements for the housing and care of animals; the essential professional, technical and personal skills for persons working in all areas of animal keeping and care; and the operation of the enforcement, authorisation and licensing system shall be determined by regulations [and, as appropriate, 'Welfare Codes', standards and guidance] of the Minister, the Ministry or the Competent Authority. This applies to all of the above activities requiring authorisation by the Minister, the Ministry or Competent Authority. With regard to authorisation procedures, these will include aspects such as: application and authorisation/licensing procedures; inspections; powers of entry and access to records; reporting and record keeping requirements; and access to animal keeping facilities.

Section 30   Nature of Enforcement

Enforcement shall consist of a mixture of: regular proactive inspections, ad-hoc inspections, general supervision, investigations into contraventions, and routine education and awareness. Inspection visits may be announced or unannounced. Preventative work shall be an important part of the enforcement process, and include education and awareness, information and advice (particularly as concerns proper animal keeping and care). Inspections shall be carried out based on risk assessment; random selection of inspection sites; regular, periodic inspections; and after becoming aware of an act done in contravention of the provisions of this Act. Inspection shall also be carried out simultaneously with the other supervision performed in relation to animal issues (as per Section 28 (3) above).

Section 31   Powers of Enforcement Bodies

(1) The bodies responsible for the enforcement of the present Act shall have access to premises, installations and equipment, vehicles, records and animals in order to review compliance with the subject Act or with any imposed prohibition to kept animals.

(2) The owners, managers or people in charge of the premises, installations and equipment, vehicles, records and animals shall enable the enforcement to be carried out; providing the required records, data, information and documentation to the Animal Welfare Inspector, and ensuring conditions for unhindered inspection.

(3) Upon the request of the Animal Welfare Inspector the owners, managers or people in charge must submit or prepare, within a specified time period, the prescribed records, data, information and documentation that the Animal Welfare Inspector requires for enforcement of the subject Act.

(4) The Competent Authorities and Animal Welfare Inspectors shall in particular have the following powers:

1. To make announced or unannounced inspection visits and to enter, examine and control, any premises, installations, equipment and vehicles used for animals; as well as to examine any animals;
2. To enter any premises or vehicle used for housing or transporting animals;
3. To require any person in or on the premises to give the inspector such assistance as is reasonable;
4. To examine any relevant records and CCTV footage, and to seize any record relating to suspected infringements;
5. To record evidence of suspected infringements; including the taking of video or photographs and witness statements;
6. To take and remove samples from the animal or premises;
7. To terminate any infringements of this Act, including any infringements of this Section, by order or by reasonable force;
8. To provide relief or to seize any animal which is kept in a condition which is causing or will lead to pain, suffering, injury, fear or distress for the animal if no effective remedy is provided and the person responsible is not willing or able to counteract the situation/abuse;
9. To arrange the painless killing of any animal for which the continuation of life would be involved with irremediable pain, suffering or distress; and
10. To arrange veterinary inspection of animals in case of doubt (of compliance with subject Act).

(5) For an animal which has as per Section 31 (4) been relieved or seized from its owner/keeper the provisions of Section 18 (1) and (2) apply accordingly.

Here regulations could be added covering the details for the relief and seizure of animals, including: The need to issue a receipt for any animal seized; the return of the animal when the requirements of this Act have been met; the period of time during which the animal will be safeguarded for the owner/keeper on his behalf before being either returned to the owner/keeper in cases where any infringements have been remedied, or the animal is finally confiscated and declared forfeited due to the expiry of this deadline.

Section 32   Improvement Notices

(1) In cases where an enforcement officer/Animal Welfare Inspector under this Act (according to Section 28) is of the opinion that a person who owns, keeps, or is in charge of an animal is failing to comply with the duties of care accorded by the provisions of this Act, or contravenes any of its provisions (particularly the requirements of Section 12 (1) - (5)), the said enforcement officer/Animal Welfare Inspector may serve to the person a notice which

1. States that he is of that opinion;
2. Specifies the respects in which he considers the person is failing to comply with the provisions of this Act;
3. Stipulates the precise steps he considers need to be taken to rectify/remedy the defects and to comply with the provisions of this Act;
4. Defines a period for the successful taking of those steps; and
5. Explains the effects of subsections (2) and (3).

(2) In cases where a notice of improvement under subsection (1) is served, no proceedings for an offence specified in this improvement notice may be instituted before the end of the period stipulated for the compliance.

(3) If the person fully complies with the requirements of the improvement notice within the specified time period, no proceedings for any offence specified in the improvement notice will be brought forward.

Section 33   Duty to Alert and Report Offences and Duty to File a Criminal Complaint

(1) Anyone who has reasons to believe that any sentient animal is exposed to mistreatment, cruelty or serious neglect with regard to environment, attention/supervision and care shall as soon as possible alert the Competent Authority or the Police. The duty to alert applies subject to the limitations of other legislation.

(2) Anyone who becomes aware that a number of wild or stray animals are exposed to sickness, injury or other abnormal suffering shall as soon as possible alert the Competent Authority or the Police.

(3) In addition, the Competent Authority shall encourage citizens to report any animal welfare infringements for further investigation and action.

(4) The Competent Authority is obliged to take action on each such alert or report: recording, verifying and investigating; and taking appropriate remedial action where necessary.

(5) The Competent Authority is obliged to file a criminal complaint when a violation according to Section 43 (1) has been committed intentionally.

Section 34   Charges and Fees

(1) As far as the subject Act does not state otherwise the enforcement is free of charge.

(2) The Minister, the Ministry and/or the Competent Authority is entitled to make provisions for the invoicing of fees or charges to cover costs of certain administrative measures, i.e. for authorisations (licenses, permits, certificates, registrations etc.), supervision, control as well as specific services under the subject Act and subordinate regulations stipulated under the Act.

Section 35   Animal Welfare Committee

(1) The Competent Authority shall appoint an Animal Welfare Committee which shall advise and assist the Minister, Ministry and/or Competent Authority on all animal welfare issues. The remit of the Committee shall include the following:

1. Assisting with the development of a national animal welfare policy and strategy; and the periodic review of such policy and strategy;
2. Providing recommendations and advice regarding animal welfare to public institutions; including new ethical, scientific and practical perspectives;
3. Providing suggestions and advice on the review of animal welfare legislation *(primary as well as secondary)*, 'Welfare Codes', standards and guidance; and enforcement and execution procedures;
4. Assisting in drafting any regulations, 'Welfare Codes', standards and guidelines with regard to the enforcement and execution of the subject Act;
5. Reviewing and assessing methods of capture, entrapment and killing of animals, in order to make recommendations to the Competent Authority on those which are deemed to be humane and in accordance with the provisions of this subject Act and should therefore be included in the permitted list; and those which do not meet this criteria and should therefore be prohibited;
6. Monitoring, reviewing and evaluating the enforcement and execution of the subject Act, and providing recommendations for any changes or enhancements necessary;
7. Providing recommendations and advice on future animal welfare research priorities;
8. Helping to develop animal welfare awareness education and campaigns for animal owners, keepers, users, and society; and
9. Administering a special fund to support programmes designed to build and develop animal welfare education, awareness and practical programmes.

Whereby this list is just a suggestion and shall not be seen as exclusive.

2) As regards the composition of the Animal Welfare Committee, it shall have a good balance of members from the fields of animal welfare, animal care, animal use, professionals and independent scientists (including veterinarians and animal behaviourists), as well as other professionals who could contribute positively to deliberations, including ethicists. Government employees may also be appointed, where animal welfare expertise and experience is present. Appointments shall be on a personal basis, and all representatives shall be selected on the grounds of expertise and sympathy to animal welfare objectives. The committee shall contain a high proportion of animal welfare experts and professionals, including representatives from leading (and/or specialist) animal welfare organisations. It shall include expertise in all major categories of animal welfare. Further rules on Committee membership shall include

1. The membership is an unpaid honorary appointment, and each member shall have an agreed deputy who may replace the member in the case of an absence.
2. The Committee shall appoint specialist sub-committees from amongst its members, covering each of the major categories of animal welfare issues:

   1) Companion animals (pets) – including stray dog and cat management;
   2) Animals kept for farming purposes – including fish farming;
   3) Animals used for experimentation – including science, research and testing;
   4) Wildlife – including pest control, and animals in zoos/aquaria;
   5) Animals used for work; and
   6) Animals used for sports, leisure and entertainment.

3. Sub-committees may invite non-officio members to contribute advice or opinions on specific issues under discussion including, but not limited to, species experts.

4. In addition to including professional ethical expertise, ethical training shall be given to all members of the Committee.

(3) The Competent Authority shall agree on detailed operating procedures and rules for the Committee, which shall include (but not be limited to) the following:

1. The committee/council is independent and shall not be bound by any instructions regarding the performance of its duties.
2. Procedures for the selection and appointment of Committee members, including the duration of the time of office and re-election arrangements.
3. Procedures for voting and decision-making.
4. Procedures for agreeing the criteria and modus operandi for authorisations, including monitoring and reviews.
5. The Committee shall be granted full access to all relevant information and facilities necessary to fulfil its obligations and meet its responsibilities.
6. Committee and Sub-Committee reports will allow minority views to be written up, and appended to the report.
7. All Committee and Sub-Committee reports (including appended minority reports) shall be openly available to the public.
8. The Committee shall prepare an annual report on its work and forward to the Minister, by [time limit] of each year. The annual report shall contain separate reports for each Sub-Committee. It shall incorporate a review of all recommendations made by the Committee, and action taken (or pending).

(4) The Sub-Committee for animal experimentation shall give opinions on ethical and animal protection issues in relation to the use of animals for experimental and educational purposes; including the establishment of an ethical review system for the review and authorisation of animal experiments.

(5) The Minister and Competent Authority is obliged to give full consideration to the views of the Committee before issuing any regulations ['Welfare Codes', standards and guidelines] under this Act.

Section 36   Animal Welfare Ombudsman

(1) The Minister or the Competent Authority shall appoint an Animal Welfare Ombudsman to act as an independent arbiter for the welfare of animals as well as their individual interests. The Ombudsman's remit will include the resolution of any complaints or conflicts concerning animal welfare matters and the correct application of this subject Act.

(2) The Animal Welfare Ombudsman shall be appointed for a period of five years, whereby a multiple number of reappointments is possible. Only such persons can be appointed who have completed appropriate professional studies and have undergone additional training in the field of animal welfare.

(3) The Animal Welfare Ombudsman shall be supported by an office [and have out-stationed representatives in each state/province/district]. The Ombudsman's office shall include animal welfare lawyers/advocates, qualified to assess and adjudicate on matters of animal welfare law, and to represent the interests of animals in court.

(4) The Competent Authority, officials, Animal Welfare Inspectors and the Animal Welfare Committee have an obligation to support the Animal Welfare Ombudsman in the exercising of his or her duties, including providing advice, assistance and access to records, statistics and data.

(5) The Animal Welfare Ombudsman and his or her staff shall be granted full access to all files of the proceedings and any relevant information relating to cases within its jurisdiction.

(6) The Animal Welfare Ombudsman shall, where necessary, arrange for his or her legal staff to represent the

individual interests of any animal as its legal agent in administrative or criminal proceedings; and assume the status of a party in any stage of the process according to the subject Act.

(7) The Animal Welfare Ombudsman is independent and not bound by any instructions in exercising his or her duties.

(8) The Animal Welfare Ombudsman and his or her staff shall not engage in any activities which are inconsistent with their sphere of duties, and/or may suggest that their position might not be impartial.

Section 37   Animal Welfare and Protection Organisations/Humane Societies

(1) The Minister, the Ministry or the Competent Authority shall involve animal welfare and protection groups/humane societies in all animal related matters. In particular, there shall be full consultation and representation in all relevant discussions and decision-making, with due weight being placed on the advice and opinions of these organisations.

(2) No organisation or individual may call itself an animal welfare or animal protection organisation (or a humane society) unless they are a registered non-profit organisation whose main mission, purpose, objectives and programmes are aimed at the promotion and development of animal welfare.

(3) The Minister, the Ministry or the Competent Authority can approve and appoint any suitably skilled and experienced animal welfare and protection organisations/humane societies to assist in the enforcement of this subject act and any provisions based on it.

(4) To qualify for such approval the organisation/society has to meet the following requirements and conditions:

1. That its main mission, purpose and objective is to promote and support animal welfare;
2. That the organisation/society simultaneously aims at serving the interest of the general public;
3. That the organisation can assure the Competent Authority that it is willing and able to fulfil all the required tasks and duties on behalf of the authorities in a professional and effective manner; and
4. That the organisation/society applies for approval in the required format.

(5) Any approved animal welfare and protection organisation/humane society may suggest suitable persons for the function of an 'Animal Welfare Inspector' according to Section 28 (7) and (8) of this subject Act. This person can be a member/employee of the said animal welfare and protection organisation/humane society, and has to possess the professional knowledge, technical skills, competence and experience to qualify for the position of an Animal Welfare Inspector.

(6) In the case of any conflicts arising for such an Animal Welfare Inspector between the duties as a member/employee of an animal welfare and protection organisation/humane society and the position of an Animal Welfare Inspector under the subject Act, the duties of an Animal Welfare Inspector according to the subject Act shall prevail.

Section 38   Animal Shelters, Animal Sanctuaries and Wildlife Rehabilitation Centres

(1) An animal shelter, animal sanctuary or wildlife rehabilitation centre may be established by a registered non-profit organisation or a natural or legal person.

(2) Animal shelters, animal sanctuaries and wildlife rehabilitation centres fall under the category of establishments

which require an authorisation in accordance with Section 29.

(3) The approval according to Section 29 shall only be granted when it is safeguarded that

1. The welfare of animals can be provided for, and all provisions of this Act met.
2. At least one person with the necessary expertise, knowledge and relevant technical skills is permanently and continuously involved in the management of the facility.
3. Proper and adequate veterinary care for the animals is provided.
4. All dogs and cats shall be spay-neutered before rehoming, to prevent further over-population, unless they are too young or physically unfit for the operation to be carried out before homing. In such cases, measures shall be taken to ensure that they are spay-neutered as soon as they are old or fit enough for this to be done without compromising their welfare. [*The costs of this may be passed on to new owners rehoming the animals.*]

(4) The management of an animal shelter, animal sanctuary or wildlife rehabilitation centre is obliged to keep records on each animal accepted into custody by date, name and place of residence of the owner or person handing over the animal (if finder, then also the location where found), type of animal, condition of health, the physical appearance and temperament of the animal, and any other facts of relevance or significance. Likewise on the occasion of discharging the animal the date, type of withdrawal, and in the case of an animal shelter the name and place of residence of the person collecting the animal, have to be registered. These records have to be kept available for a period of three years and can be requested for inspection by the authorities at any reasonable time.

(5) No organisation, facility or premises may call itself an animal shelter, animal sanctuary or wildlife rehabilitation centre, or imply that it is such an establishment, unless it has been licensed and authorised as such by the competent authority.

(6) Only registered non-profit organisations shall be entitled to seek and receive public donations, contributions and sponsorship for their work as an animal shelter, animal sanctuary or wildlife rehabilitation centre.

(7) In addition: Authorisation of the Minister responsible, the Ministry or the Competent Authority to adopt any regulations [and establish, as appropriate, 'Welfare Codes', standards and guidance] in this context.

Section 39   Veterinarians and Para-Veterinarians

(1) Veterinarians and para-veterinarians shall at all times use their scientific knowledge and veterinary skills to protect the health and welfare of any animal committed to their care, and for the prevention and relief of animal suffering.

(2) Regardless of any commercial or professional interest, veterinarians and para-veterinarians shall always put the welfare of the animal first.

(3) Where veterinarians and para-veterinarians have any evidence or suspicions that this law has not been complied with in any way, they are obliged to report this to the Competent Authority without delay.

(4) Animal welfare shall be included in the curriculum of any veterinary university or other tertiary or further education establishment offering veterinary or para-veterinary training in the country.

(5) Animal welfare shall be included as a Continuing Professional Development (CPD) course for veterinarians.

Section 40   Animal Welfare Research

The Competent Authority shall support the development of national research on animal welfare and, in particular, the development of research programmes designed to consider national animal welfare priorities, and the applicability of international animal welfare research to prevailing national and local situations. The Competent Authority shall also support the research and development of alternatives to the use of animals in research.

Section 41   Consumer Information

(1) Consumers shall be provided with clear information on the animal welfare criteria or implications of all products of animal origin, and all products that have used animals in their manufacture or testing. This shall be adequate and sufficient to empower consumers to make informed purchasing choices.

(2) Any information provided to inform consumers about the positive animal welfare criteria or credentials of products, or that could be deemed to signify positive animal welfare criteria or credentials, shall be accurate and not misleading in any manner. This applies whether on labels, signs, banners or otherwise; and whether presented in writing or pictorially.

Section 42   Animal Welfare Measurement and Impact Assessment

(1) An animal welfare impact assessment shall be carried out in all cases where there is the likelihood of policies, laws, programmes or activities adversely affecting the welfare or lives of animals.

(2) With regard to policy and legislative arenas, the assessment shall cover the need for coherence and consistency between other relevant policy areas and the welfare needs of animals. This brings an obligation to ensure that the welfare of animals is taken into account in all relevant areas of government policy and regulation.

(3) Where these assessments indicate the potential to cause adverse animal welfare impacts, or danger to animal lives, a full ethical review shall be conducted before any decisions are taken on the proposed policies, laws, programmes or activities; subsequently all measures shall be taken to avoid or counter such impacts or damage.

(4) The Competent Authority shall, after consulting with stakeholders, develop animal welfare indicators. These shall include both 'input' and 'outcome' measurements to be used each time there is an inspection or enforcement visit to any animal user or establishment. Such indicators shall be regularly reviewed, and updated on the basis of the latest scientific knowledge and ethical advances in the animal welfare field.

(5) Statistics shall be prepared based on different animal uses, in order to identify any welfare problems in specific animal industries or uses. These statistics shall be analysed annually, and made publically available.

(6) Where inspection and enforcement visits and/or statistics indicate a particular concern with any animal industry or use, then measures shall be taken to resolve this without delay. In cases where it is not possible to resolve such problems, then the animal use in question should be prohibited in order to prevent further animal suffering.

CHAPTER 6: PENAL AND FINAL/CONCLUDING PROVISIONS

Section 43   Penal and Administrative Fine Provisions

(1) Liable of a criminal offence and on conviction to imprisonment for a period not exceeding a *level 4 offence* and to a fine according to a *level 4 offence* shall be who

1. Kills any sentient animal without a sound justification;
2. Inflicts on any sentient animal
   1) Deliberately, intentionally or out of brutality pain or suffering; or
   2) Prolonged or repeated pain or suffering;
3. Sets any animal on another animal with the intent that a sentient animal experiences pain, suffering or injury;
4. Performs an act of bestiality with a sentient animal; or
5. Abandons any sentient animal that is unlikely to survive in freedom.

(2) An administrative offence is committed by any person who deliberately or negligently violates against the provisions of Sections 7, 8, 10, 11 or any of the Sections listed under Chapter 3 (Keeping of Animals/Care of Animals) and Chapter 4 (Specific Categories of Animal Use).

1. In minor cases the punishment for such an administrative offence will be *classified as a level 1 offence.*
2. In serious cases the punishment for such an administrative offence will be a fine *according to a level 2 offence.*
3. For aggravated infringements as well as repeated offences the fine will be *rated as a level 3 offence.*

The separate banding list could then read as follows:

Level 1 offence – minor infringements.;
Level 2 offence – serious infringements;
Level 3 offence – aggravated infringements as well as repeated offences; and
Level 4 offences – imprisonment and/or fine for criminal offences

The currency amounts for each of these bandings will be determined by the Competent Authority in Regulations (or as published periodically in the Official Gazette).

(3) Any attempt is already punishable.

Section 44 Prohibition of Keeping Animals or of Having Contact with Animals and Forfeiture

(1) The authorities can prohibit a person who has been convicted by the courts with final legal effect for an unlawful act against Section 43 (1) or who has been punished by the administrative authorities for an offence against Sections 7, 8, 10, 11 or any of the Sections listed under Chapter 3 (Keeping of Animals/Care of Animals) and Chapter 4 (Specific Categories of Animal Use) from keeping, breeding or trading animals or from having any contact with animals in general or with a particular species of animal for a certain period of time or permanently if there is the risk that this person will continue or again violate Section 43 (1) or contravene against the provisions of the Sections 7, 8, 10, 11 or any of the Sections listed under Chapter 3 (Keeping of Animals/Care of Animals) and Chapter 4 (Specific Categories of Animal Use).

(2) The same applies if a person is in other aspects not capable of keeping or breeding animals.

(3) Animals which have been the object/subject of the punishable conduct may be confiscated and declared forfeited; in which case the provisions of Section 18 (1) apply accordingly.

(4) Similarly, in cases where a person is disqualified or prohibited from keeping, breeding, trading or working with animals (or with a particular species of animal), then all animals (or all animals of this particular species) in his/her care should be confiscated and declared forfeited; in which case the provisions of Section 18 (1) shall also apply accordingly.

Section 45 Further Aspects

- Implementation of further approvals as required;
- Introduction of additional licenses and permits as needed;
- Authorisation to issue further regulations as required;
- Consideration of financial implications, e.g. budgetary systems, expenditure compensated through revenues like charging fees for certain administrative measures etc.;
- Compulsory vocational education for certain animal related occupations and further training;
- Revision of the Act on a regular basis to remain up-to-date and using current 'best practice';
- For certain measures phase-out and phase-in periods should be integrated, where appropriate and sensible; and
- Revocation of existing 'Animal Protection/Welfare Act' and replacement with the new Animal Welfare Act.

PART 3

EXPLANATORY
NOTES

To facilitate the understanding of this Act as well as for information purposes – aspects which, from the authors' point of view, may need additional clarification have been further expanded below.

CHAPTER 1: PRELIMINARY PROVISIONS

Section 1 — Title, Commencement and Conflicting Provisions

As regards commencement, the Act could be brought into operation on a given date in the future, at a time which would permit the Competent Authority to begin implementation without delay. As the Act envisages progressive implementation this need not be a lengthy delay. However, where provisions will necessitate work and investment to amend animal keeping/husbandry/handling systems (such as animal housing/enclosures, fixtures/fittings or equipment), then a phase-in period can be stipulated in the relevant provision. Experience elsewhere has indicated that this must be stressed to be mandatory, with stringent express penalties for lack of compliance (otherwise animal industries will not use the period concerned to make the necessary adaptations).

Section 2 — Objectives

Lays out the overall objectives of the Act. It is important that these objectives include the progressive development of humane attitudes, as well as protection of animal welfare.

Section 3 — Support for Animal Welfare

Section 3 (1): Obliges the state with the mandate to promote and support animal welfare and the development of humane attitudes, ideologically as well as materially. This not only gives the government the responsibility for educating, informing and sensitising the public, but also for providing the financial resources needed to support the development of animal welfare and humane attitudes.

It is the nation's as well as its society's duty to instigate a change of attitude towards animal welfare concerns by informing and educating its people so every individual is able to take an ethical and moral decision on their relationship to their fellow creatures. The state is therefore bound to take steps to progressively counteract any deficiencies in its society's knowledge, understanding and awareness which prevent the achievement of the protection of the lives and welfare of animals.

Section 3 (2): It is envisaged that this work would include

- Research

Supporting and (co-)funding research in areas such as: animal welfare (for example, humane forms of animal keeping), the application of indigenous knowledge to improve animal welfare (including use of traditional/adapted breeds), alternatives to animal experiments, and the development of humane attitudes.

The establishment of a strong and dynamic institutional relationship between animal welfare scientists and regulatory agencies is an important precursor to the development of good animal welfare legislation.

- Good Practice Development

The collection and dissemination of animal welfare good practice: pilot projects, case studies, research and cooperation (within and outside of the country) – thus facilitating the application of nationally appropriate best practice.

- Training and Capacity Building

Support and funding for training and capacity building (including the provision of guidance) on animal welfare where most needed, e.g.: policy officials, enforcement officers/police officers and extension workers.
Support (including technical support/expertise and political support) would also be needed for similar training and capacity building for other relevant stakeholders, such as NGOs (including both animal welfare organisations and others working on animal issues), veterinarians (and other animal health workers, such as para-vets), animal owners/keepers and animal industries (including farmers/farmers groups, traders, transporters, handlers, and slaughterhouses).

- Education

The introduction of programmes at schools, further and higher education bodies (such as: veterinary universities and agricultural colleges).

- Public Awareness

The introduction of communication and public awareness programmes including: events and actions, use of international days (for example, World Animal Day, World Wildlife Day and World Rabies Day) and use of the mass media.

- Animal Welfare Organisations/NGOs

Supporting and encouraging the establishment and effective running of NGOs engaging in animal welfare matters, i.e. animal welfare and protection organisations, such as SPCAs. Also, funding (or co-funding) of services provided in connection with this Animal Welfare Act.

In the context of financial support, consideration could be given to including a financial clause in this paragraph specifying the extent of the state's obligations. Without such a specific provision, the state may not be able to limit or restrict the extent of its liability, or prioritise its engagement based on its assessment of need, relative urgency and importance, and the weighting of interests on a case-by-case basis. There will clearly be areas where the state should have primary responsibility; and others where the obligation should be passed to other stakeholders (for example, animal industries – where the costs incurred in complying with this Act should be part and parcel of their operating costs).

Section 4   Scope of Application

The aim of this Act is the protection of the lives and welfare of animals. Animal protection is aimed at safeguarding the animal and preserving it from harm, injury, and negative impacts and actions. Thus, by definition, animal protection constitutes and implements specifically targeted assistance for each and every animal. In principle, both the concepts of animal welfare and animal protection would incorporate the protection of life, and therefore the provisions of any animal welfare law should also embrace each animal as an individual regardless of the species, assumed possible inferiority as a species or the species value or detriment (for instance as a 'pest') for the human. Indeed, the major distinction between animal welfare and conservation is this very care for each individual animal, as opposed to the species.

For avoidance of doubt, we have defined an 'animal' as any mammal, bird, reptile, amphibian, fish, insect or other multi-cellular organism that is not a plant or fungi.

Whilst a number of contemporary animal welfare laws – such as the UK's Animal Welfare Act 2006 and the Swiss Tierschutzgesetz (Animal Welfare Act) of 2005 – continue to restrict their range of application to vertebrates alone, others espouse the principle of comprehensive and unconditional protection of life – as can be found, for instance, in the current and exemplary German (Tierschutzgesetz 2006) and Austrian (Tierschutzgesetz 2005) animal welfare laws (although certain sections of these laws apply only to vertebrates (Germany), and vertebrates, cephalopods and decapods (Austria)). The New Zealand Act (Animal Welfare Act 1999 – reprint 1 January 2014) also has a wide definition of 'animal'. A wider scope is favoured. Even if science has not yet demonstrated a comparable capability to suffer or feel pain in some non-vertebrates, they can experience harm and damage, their physical integrity can be impaired and their welfare could be detrimentally affected.

Another factor that is often considered in relation to the scope of an animal welfare law is whether this should cover animals living in the wild, as well as those in captivity. The inclusion of wild-living animals is favoured, as human actions and activities can affect the welfare of these animals as well as those directly under the custody or care of people.

The argument is sometimes advanced that wild animals living in wilderness areas should be left alone. Whilst we agree with this in principle, in practice the situation with wild animals is more complex. There are few truly wild habitats left in the world where animals can live their lives without being affected by human activities: Not only are animals' habitats encroached by human expansion and their lives affected by human-caused factors such as climate change; but also their territories are often entered by humans, or criss-crossed by roads, railways, farms, power lines, fences, and even country borders. These factors are also causing more wild animals to voluntarily enter into areas of human habitation, where our lives become inextricably linked and entwined, and the way in which we deal with wild animal encounters directly affects their welfare – and sometimes their lives. Hence there is an ethical imperative to include these animals in the scope of the law: The question is not so much whether an animal is living in the wild or in the custody or care of people; but rather whether there is the possibility of human actions affecting the welfare of that individual animal. This is why the definition covers all animals regardless of the animal being domestic or wild.

Where the objective is to develop a prudent and morally responsible human-animal relationship on a compassionate level (in terms of principles, education and changing attitudes) and an ethically-based system of animal welfare, which is comprehensive and future-orientated, then the basic scope of legal protection for animals should be all-embracing and cover all animals indiscriminately. Thus, the decision for this Act is to cover all non-human animals, using a wide definition of 'animal'. The decision to focus Chapters 5 and 6 (on enforcement and penalties) on sentient animals was based on reasons of practicality and the effective targeting of enforcement and prosecution resources. However, if this approach is followed, then the precautionary principle should always be applied - as science is showing that an increasing number of species of animals are sentient than was previously supposed.

Section 5   Definitions

In many legal orders it is common practice to give a catalogue of definitions to help with the application of the law and to avoid – as far as possible – any misinterpretations of the wording of the law by its users. These definitions serve as clarifications and often prove to be exceedingly valuable tools in the implementation and execution of an act. Some laws have very elaborate definitions which do not necessarily serve their intended purpose, particularly when they expound at great length on common place expressions and established terms. Preference should be given to specifying crucial essentials and substantive differences, especially when any further or different legal consequences are drawn from the distinctions: for instance, the classification of animals in certain groups such as 'wild animals', 'farmed animals' or 'animals used for work', 'companion animals' etc., or to describe in more detail a

Competent Authority or the attributes of an Animal Welfare Inspector.

The list given here should not be seen as conclusive, but is just a proposal which can be contracted or expanded according to need, requirements and desire.

Section 5 Pt. 2: It is understood that 'Animal Protection' could be implemented by practical, legal or formal measures to prevent suffering and preserve liberties, interests and/or rights.

Section 5 Pt. 4: In regard to 'Animal Shelter', the definition specifically states that this should be operated by a charitable, non-profit animal welfare organisation, both in order to distinguish a shelter from a government/municipal facility and to prevent private enterprises from using this terminology to solicit donations for private animal collections.

Section 5 Pt. 28: The definition of veterinarian can be amended to suit the prevailing system, i.e. whether veterinarians are registered, certified or licensed (or indeed any other form of authorisation) to practice as a veterinarian.

The list is not comprehensive and could for example be broadened to also incorporate some more abstract and ambiguous terms like

- *Dignity – Inherent worth of the animal that has to be respected when dealing with it. If any strain imposed on the animal cannot be justified by overriding interests, this constitutes a disregard for the animal's dignity. Strain is deemed to be present in particular if pain, suffering or harm is inflicted on the animal, if it is exposed to anxiety or humiliation, if there is major interference with its appearance or its abilities or if it is excessively instrumentalised.*

The term 'dignity' is used in the Swiss Animal Welfare Act (Tierschutzgesetz 2005).

Section 6   Fundamental Principles of Animal Welfare

The fundamental principles underlying this Act have been reiterated here in order to ensure that they are well understood and promulgated along with the law. Also, there is an obligation for these to be considered by every person using or applying the Act and by any supporting secondary legislation, i.e. regulations, as well as 'Welfare Codes' and standards. This specifically includes cases where the Act/auxiliary regulations [and, as appropriate, 'Welfare Codes', standards and guidance] are subject to interpretation.

We consider the principle of the 3Rs, which were first introduced in Russell and Burch's 1959 book 'The Principles of Humane Experimental Techniques', to be ethically sound and practical to apply. As well as being internationally recognised, these are prominently highlighted as a guiding principle in European Union (EU) Directive 2010/63/EU on the protection of animals used for scientific purposes (see: For instance, Pt. (10), (11) and (13), and Articles 4 and 13 of Directive 2010/63/EU).

It is logical to extend the 3R principles to all other areas of commercial animal use (with appropriate minor textual amendments), particularly where there is any doubt that the welfare needs of the animals can be met. Indeed, they are already being applied in many areas. For example, as regards livestock production,

- Reduction – 'Eat Less Meat' programmes, 'Meat Free' days (Mondays or Fridays) etc.;
- Refinement – Introduction of free range and organic systems; and
- Replacement – The development of cultured meat and vegetarian meat replacements.

In all cases, replacement should be the ultimate goal.

CHAPTER 2: GENERAL PROVISIONS

Whilst the primary purpose of this Act is the development of a humane ethic and positive 'duty of care', the following provisions mainly relating to the general human-animal relationship are established at the outset to categorically prohibit certain unacceptable acts of cruelty.

Section 7   Prohibition of Cruelty to Animals

Section 7 (1): This Axiom contains the core elements of an offence against this law. It is a general clause explicitly prohibiting the infliction/causing of pain, suffering or injury on an animal, or exposing an animal to illness and disease or to fear and distress, without 'sound justification' (in terms of any overriding reason of human or animal welfare), whereby 'sound justification' means there is a factual/objective justification or a legitimate interest for the act or omission, in other words the conduct must be in regard to the reason as well as to the expedient used and the extent of the encroachment vindicated.

This norm protects all animals and makes no distinction between owned animals and animals which are not under the ambit or care of people. The tort itself can be committed by everybody. Both wilful and negligent commitments of the offence are covered.

The wording of the general prohibition clause has been carefully considered, and a decision made to express this as a prima facie prohibition against the infliction of any pain, suffering, injury or the exposure to illness and disease or to fear or distress - with the only exception to this being over-riding reasons of human or animal welfare (with 'sound justification' explained above). This is considered the only way of complying with the internationally-recognised Five Freedoms, which have been included as fundamental principles of this Act. The use of any wide qualification of the prohibition, such as 'unnecessary' or 'unavoidable' has been dismissed as such terms are frequently used to justify the breach of clauses protecting the welfare of animals when balanced against any common commercial practices or economic needs. In our view, this approach does not meet the spirit of the Five Freedoms, or the moral imperative to safeguard the welfare of each animal.
[However, if consideration is given to including any qualifying terms, then (as regards 'pain, suffering or injury') the term 'avoidable' is considered preferable to the term 'unnecessary', which has already caused many interpretive problems in practice.]

Similarly, deliberation has been given to the possibility of including the qualification 'significant' in relation to 'fear' in some of the specified provisions detailed in Section 7 (2) *(see below)*, as it was recognised that in some cases fear could be fleeting and also triggered in response to an imagined threat (as well as a real threat). In such cases, it would be considered disproportionate to prosecute. However, the qualifier was omitted in order to meet the principles of the Five Freedoms. At an earlier stage the qualifier 'significant' was likewise rejected in relation to 'distress', because 'distress' was considered to have more of a fundamental impact on the welfare of the animal.
[However, if consideration is given to including any qualifying terms, in regard to 'fear' then the term 'significant' is considered preferable to either 'avoidable' or 'unnecessary', for the reasons given above. As regards 'distress' no qualifier is considered acceptable.]

Section 7 (2): Contains a list of specified general prohibitions which are not subject to negotiation. These provisions deal with the human's incumbent responsibility for his/her actions towards the animal as a fellow being. Thus they stipulate the basic mandatory principles of human conduct towards the animal, providing the imperative guidelines which would form the basis of any further and more specific regulations [and, as appropriate, 'Welfare Codes', standards and guidance].

Still, this list of 26 gross violations is neither final nor conclusive, and can be extended by the inclusion of further serious general prohibitions if the legislator feels this would be preferable for reasons of clarity and detail. However, it should be born in mind that not all contingencies can be comprehensively covered at an early stage of law development, so it is often preferable to include wider general provisions, as opposed to a greater number of provisions containing more specific details. The aim is to provide a framework law which establishes major principles, which cover the widest possible variety of circumstances, but remains transparent and accessible.

The order of these violations should not be deemed to be indicative of the severity of the individual act or infringement, i.e. the position in the list of provisions does not reflect the severity of the breach (and should not be interpreted as the higher the more serious, and the lower the less serious the offence).

To Pt. 11: Some of the provisions in Section 7 (2) are general in nature, and will need to be more specific and tightly drafted in regulations. For example, this provision on tethering could specify the minimum length of any tether and its type (e.g. a running lead which moves freely and enables a dog to run along its length without danger of entanglement).

To Pt. 20: The Animal Welfare Committee will compile a list of traps and catching devices which are authorised, as well as define which poisons are allowable in which circumstances (positive list). When carrying out their review, they will also clarify which do not meet their criteria, and therefore should be prohibited.

To Pt. 23: This provision safeguards domestic or companion animals from abandonment in all circumstances. It also prevents the abandonment/release of non-indigenous wildlife in recognition of the fact that these are not adapted to survive in the alien environment and may adversely affect the welfare of native wildlife and the balance of nature/biodiversity. As regards indigenous wildlife, the provision against abandonment/release applies in cases where they have not been fully rehabilitated or where there are any doubts about their ability to survive. This is to prevent abandonment or irresponsible release back into the wild and/or release into unsuitable territory (for example, into alien habitat and/or in close proximity to human habitation).
'Founded reasons' (to doubt an animal's ability to survive in the territory to which it is being released) would include examples such as: the case of an injured wild animal which has not been successfully rehabilitated to adapt to a life in the wild; or a wild animal being released into unsuitable or dangerous territory.

To Pt. 26: This provision is in particular aimed at prohibiting sexual actions for the purpose of sexual gratification, perversion, recreation, entertainment or abuse. 'Unnatural offences' against animals, such as 'carnal knowledge of an animal'/sodomy/bestiality, are sometimes included in a country's Penal Code. It has been incorporated here in this framework Act, to ensure that all criminal offences against animals are covered in one law. This may necessitate further discussion, and possibly an amendment of the Penal Code.

Section 8   Prohibited Interventions Performed on Animals

Today's legal requirements in connection with interventions performed on animals have to conform to a number of important (and often recently established) norms. It is necessary that these norms are prominently reflected in any new regulations [and, as appropriate, 'Welfare Codes', standards and guidance]. The underlying principles include securing the integrity and well-being of the animal.

Clearly interventions have to be permitted for therapeutic or diagnostic purposes, where these are likely to be in the interests of the animal's health and welfare. An exception has also been permitted for expert markings/identification, where this is carried out in accordance with legal regulations. This is currently considered acceptable for purposes of animal management and traceability, but may be superseded by more welfare-friendly methods in the future – in which case the situation can be amended by regulatory means, as opposed to an amendment of this act.

Any intervention to create a transgenic animal is categorically prohibited, as not only might this have a detrimental impact on the animal or the animal's progeny; but would also infringe the intrinsic value and integrity of the animal.

Non-therapeutic mutilations are strictly prohibited, with the exception of a limited number of specified exemptions, for example, to prevent reproduction or to indicate a neutered stray animal by the tipping of an ear *(see Section 8 (3) for details).*

In addition and as a brief summary of Section 8, three main focus points alone would justify any intervention which might cause any pain for the animal: a medical indication must be established and then the intervention may only be performed under effective anaesthesia and in compliance with the obligation that the procedure including the pre-sedation, the post-operative treatment of pain and with non-steroidal anti-inflammatory drugs must be carried out by a qualified veterinarian.

Section 9   Prohibition of Killing Animals

Section 9 (1): Initially animal protection legislation concentrated mainly on the prohibition of animal cruelty. The unjustified (please see also explanation of 'sound justification' in the Explanatory Notes to Section 7 (1) above) killing of a vertebrate was only made a punishable offence from the second half of the last century (for example, by Germany in the 70s). In principle, following an ethical approach, a comprehensive protection of life should be guaranteed for every individual animal – thus the general interdiction of killing an animal should be explicitly included in the law. However, in order to enable practical and progressive implementation this prohibition is dealt with by providing limited permission for the killing of animals, as stated in accordance with provisions stipulating an exception from this rule and offering an express authorisation, for example in connection with the killing/slaughter for the production of meat or for reasons of disease or 'pest' control. It is also worth remembering that 'sound justification' will be partly dependent on current social and cultural norms, and may therefore change over time (for example, killing of animals for food may currently be considered an accepted justification, but this may not be the case in future, for instance, when meat substitutes and test-tube grown meat are widely available and accepted).

Section 9 (2): The inclusion of a categorical ban on killing of a companion animal, and in particular of dogs and cats, does not seem superfluous within this concept. These animals have been domesticated to hold a special relationship with humans, rather than for any economic purposes. Thus no justification is able to override these strict legal rules.
Countries may consider adding other animals to this list – for example, wildlife (such as turtles or tortoises) for which there may already be a ban on killing in a wildlife law.

Section 9 (3): A categorical ban on the killing of any animal in order to provide entertainment has also been included. This is for avoidance of doubt – here again no justification is able to override these strict legal rules.

Section 9 (4): Here consideration could also be given to imposing a prohibition of killing an animal in a public place/space (like a market, a street, a square etc.) and of killing an animal in the sight or view of another conscious animal.

Section 10 Prohibition of Passing on, Selling, Offering for Sale, Purchasing or Possessing Certain Animals (Doomed Animals)

Section 10 (1): Another exception from Section 9's prohibition to kill any animal is covered in Section 10 in association with doomed animals. This is the case when the continuation of life would be connected with irremediable pain, suffering, agony, torment or distress, which would represent an unreasonable and unacceptable burden for an animal. In such cases the law requires the immediate humane killing of the animal concerned. This first sub-section prohibits the passing on, selling, offering for sale or purchase of such animals.

Section 10 (2): Further prohibition has been included covering the possession of any animal, without reasonable cause, which is suffering irremediable pain, agony, torment or distress. This is necessary for purposes of consistency of approach – to ensure that owned animals do not suffer similar unreasonable and unacceptable burdens; requiring the immediate humane killing of such animals. This can assist animal welfare in practical ways, for example, in cases where producers retain a suffering animal until it reaches its slaughter weight, or where owners or keepers of companion animals still keep them alive even though they are doomed and their welfare is seriously impaired.

Section 11 Obligation to Grant First Aid

Evidently, there are discrepancies in concepts and views regarding an obligation to extend first aid to an animal and these are to a certain degree attributable to differences between legal systems. In Austria for instance according to § 9 Tierschutzgesetz (Animal Welfare Act) of 2005 someone "who has recognisably hurt or jeopardized an animal shall, to the extent he can reasonably be expected to do so, grant the necessary first aid to the animal". The new Norwegian Animal Welfare Act of 2010 goes even further and speaks in its § 4. 'Duty to help' provision of the general public, i.e. "anybody who discovers an animal which is obviously sick, injured, or helpless, shall as far as possible help the animal", so here no perpetrator situation is required any more.

As the aspiration is to compile a forward-looking and all-embracing piece of legislation, the Norwegian approach is definitely seen as among the most progressive and considerate practices and thus preferred.

Section 11 (1): Obliges everyone, and not just those causing an accident or a hazardous situation, to render an animal first aid and care as needed, or to arrange for such first aid and care and/or diagnosis and treatment. However, this legal duty is slightly limited as it falls under the precondition that the person concerned can reasonably be expected to act and comply with this obligation.

Section 11 (2): Obliges the owner or keeper of an animal to provide a sick, injured or distressed animal with diagnosis and appropriate treatment without any delay: Where necessary, veterinary advice must be sought. For avoidance of doubt: The primary duty of care falls upon the owner or keeper of the animal. However, it is recognised that in emergency situations, as above, the owner or keeper may not be on hand or available to carry out such duties.

To Chapter 2 – Aspects still to be given further consideration:

- From the perspective of creating an objective ranking for the above mentioned provisions further consideration could be given to whether the 'Prohibition of Killing Animals' (Section 9) – as the more serious infringement – should be positioned before the 'Prohibition of Cruelty to Animals' (Section 7). The traditional classification of cruelty to animals utilised here and thus systematically located before the actual tort of killing an animal, results from legal-historical reasons; as originally animal cruelty was the primary determinant of the real legitimacy of animal protection, and thus constituted the central focus and objective of animal protection laws. Nowadays this no longer applies; and in most of the more recent examples of animal welfare laws the unjustified killing of a vertebrate is now seen as a punishable offence.

- Another fundamental consideration is whether to include, in the appropriate position, a general paragraph giving the Minister or the Competent Authority the authorisation to adopt any regulations [supplemented as necessary by 'Welfare Codes', standards and guidance] in order to provide further interpretation or detail in support of certain provisions.

CHAPTER 3: KEEPING OF ANIMALS/CARE OF ANIMALS

Animal keeping is one of the issues which no longer focuses exclusively on the human-animal relationship, but warrants additional specified requirements for the treatment of those animals which are in the hands of humans and thus are subject to the imperative of increased consideration and care on the part of humans. It is irrelevant in this context whether the animal in question is in human custody on a permanent basis or only temporarily, as for instance in the case of animal transportation (as per the definition of 'keeper').

A.   General Regulations

Section 12   Principles of Keeping Animals

Section 12 (1): The 'Principles of Keeping Animals' serve first and foremost to safeguard the animal's well-being. The most important relevant consideration, with reference to the ethical guiding principles of the law, is that the animal has to be treated and kept commensurate and appropriate to its species-specific and individual needs and requirements: meaning supplied with appropriate food/nourishment, liquid and care, as well as a suitable accommodation, sufficient room for exercise and also the possibility for social interaction - without exception. In addition, the animal shall be able to live without pain, suffering, injury, fear or distress.

To Pt. 1: This provision would cover not only the need to provide food and drink of an appropriate type and quantity, but also to ensure that it is accessible (for example, in the case of drink this should be presented in a manner that enables an animal to drink naturally e.g. from a drinking nipple for young animals) and also appropriate from a behavioural point of view (for example, permitting foraging where such behaviour is natural).

Section 12 (2): This provision will prohibit the use of housing systems that fail to comply with the animal welfare requirements detailed in Section 12 (1) and any prescribed minimum standards. It is considered good practice for the Competent Authority to establish more detailed minimum standards for housing systems, in order to equip the industry with more concrete advice and guidance in this regard (which is particularly valuable where potentially high investments are at stake). Thus Section (7) vests the Competent Authority with the necessary authorisation to provide such guidance – see below.

Section 12 (3) and (4): In accordance with agreed animal welfare principles and the latest animal welfare regulations, any permanent chaining or tethering should be completely prohibited. Any chaining or tethering should only be a temporary measure to safeguard the animal's welfare. Ideally, all chaining or tethering should be inadmissible, if other methods of restraint are available which are more welfare-friendly.

Dogs should not be tethered more than temporarily (for example to restrain them when out e.g. on a visit to the veterinarian), or on a running chain which permits free movement (a walled garden would be preferable, if available – but it is recognised that this is not always possible or practical). However, this provision would in no way prevent a dog from being walked on a leash.

Section 12 (6): An animal within the social unit of a family is often appreciated as an integral part of this emotional coexistence of spouses, children and pet. Thus there is also an increasing number of disputes over ownership of animals, particularly companion animals when marriages or partnerships break up. These have the potential to significantly affect the welfare of the animals, unless resolved in a manner which prioritises the welfare of the individual animal. Therefore custody of the animal has to be granted to the person who is willing to assume the duties of the keeper of the animal and at the same time is in the best position to ensure the well-being of the animal.

Section 12 (7): In relation to Section (2) above, in addition to providing authorisation for the Competent Authority to determine minimum standards for housing systems, this Section provides powers for the requirement of prior authorisation of systems. This is an effective method of ensuring that only systems which meet the given criteria are introduced. Such a scheme can be established for any new systems, and existing systems given a phase-out period, during which they have to be adapted or replaced if necessary in order to comply. The prior authorisation scheme prevents the (costly) acquisition of new systems which fail to comply, and are unacceptable from a welfare perspective, i.e. it provides clarity and reassurance regarding the acceptability of new housing systems before any investment is made.
[Experience shows that lack of clear specifications and guidance causes the industry to rally against change, when it has made significant investments in non-compliant systems.]

Section 13   Qualifications of the Animal Keeper

Section 13 (1): Although at times it would seem very welcome to impose stricter requirements on the animal keeper than usually legally mandatory, in general everybody has a right to keep animals provided that they are capable of complying with the law. An exception from this entitlement is made in the case that the animal keeper has been banned from keeping animals due to prior violations of the subject Act or any other legislation.

Section 13 (2): The demand for expertise in the keeping of animals is only recently being introduced into animal welfare legislation. This was also included in the OIE's General Principles (Chapter 7.1. of the Terrestrial Animal Health Code, Article 7.1.4 Pt. 11) which states that: "Owners and handlers should have sufficient skill and knowledge to ensure that animals are treated in accordance with these principles". It has long been recognised that this plays an important contribution to the well-being of animals. Clearly, a number of violations of the law could be prevented if animal keepers had greater knowledge and understanding of humane keeping, handling and care of animals in connection with their tasks and duties. Thus it is considered essential that this aspect is covered in any modern animal welfare law.
There is no general requirement within this law for a formally recognised proof of knowledge and skills, because this was not felt to be universally necessary (for example, in the case of companion animals). However, it is recognised that this provision would leave some scope for interpretation, and that this could be particularly problematic in commercial transactions (whereby an animal owner or keeper would need to prove 'due diligence' in complying with the law). Thus it is considered that this aspect would need to be realised and implemented by statutory regulations and legal obligations.
Also, initiatives supporting and promoting information, awareness and education/training are core issues to be followed up simultaneously.

Section 13 (3) and (4): It is every keeper's obligation to ensure that he/she has access to the relevant information, advice and education/training. In a commercial situation, it is envisaged that a company/employer would provide this for its employees (either by employing those already qualified, or by providing the necessary training/qualification). The provision requiring animal owners to ensure that keepers have the necessary knowledge and required skills would cover both the situation where an animal keeping enterprise is obliged to comply with these requirements (by ensuring that employees were properly trained/qualified), and where an owner of any animal gives his/her animal into the keeping of another (for example, a transporter, slaughterhouse, boarding kennel etc.). In such circumstances, the owner would need to satisfy him/herself that the keeper in question was appropriately trained/qualified (thus safeguarding the welfare of his/her animal).

Section 13 (5): This provision will need to be tailored to local jurisdictions (as some countries may have a set age at which young people are no longer considered minors requiring guardian's consent).

Section 14   Care in Case of Illness or Injury

This injunction makes provisions against any indifference and negligence rendered towards an ill or injured animal, and wants to clearly foster a sense of responsibility and empathy for the needy and vulnerable animal. Animals which show signs of pain or distress, but are not evidently ill or injured, also need to be inspected, and the cause of their pain or distress identified. In cases where the cause of the animal's pain or distress cannot be identified and/or where the owner/keeper is not able to remedy the animal's illness or injury, then veterinary attention must be provided.
The duty to separate a sick animal is not only in the interest of its own well-being, but also serves to avoid the risk of infecting other healthy animals.

Further aspects to be stressed: Here again consideration could be given to including a paragraph in each section giving the Minister or the Competent Authority the authorisation to adopt any regulations [and, as appropriate, establish 'Welfare Codes', standards and guidance] in order to provide further interpretation or detail in support of certain provisions (or, for example, to allow for exceptions).

B.   Special Regulations
Section 15   Principles of Animal Breeding

Breeding should only exculpate a selection for physically and mentally healthy animals and thus support and encourage positive and natural development, and not bioengineering in its most negative spin-offs. Consequently inhumane breeding practices or breeding for unhealthy traits are prohibited. Equally the concept of breeding and releasing transgenic animals encounters strong resistance and opposition, and legitimate concerns about unintended detrimental consequences: Thus countries should also consider a ban of these methods.

Section 15 (4): Breeding for positive welfare traits is encouraged. However, animals should not be purposefully bred for adaptation to industrial farming systems; as when systems do not provide good welfare, then it is the system that should be changed, and not the animal.

Section 16   Keeping of Animals within the Scope of Business Activities

Section 16 (1): As with some of the before mentioned activities, the keeping and breeding of animals for business purposes falls under the categories requiring an authorisation in accordance with Section 29. Each jurisdiction can decide whether this should in the form of registration or licensing. Animal shelters and wildlife rehabilitation centres have not been included in the list because they are usually not-for-profit enterprises, and have been dealt with separately under Section 38.

Consideration would be given to excluding dog walkers and dog/cat sitters from this provision, where this is carried out as a 'pocket-money business' (like baby-sitting), and not a regular activity run on a profit-making business model (such as a kennel, dog hotel etc.).

An authorisation system enables the Competent Authority to control and restrict certain activities, as well as facilitating the monitoring of businesses. For example, if there is an overpopulation problem with dogs or cats, then they could decide to prohibit commercial breeding of these animals; or severely restrict and control the number of authorised breeders. Intensive breeding of companion animals (such as in 'puppy mills' or 'puppy farms' should be expressly prohibited, and no authorisations given for such activities).

Section 16 (2): This section covers the fundamental requirements of the authorisation process. Further requirements could be added by regulations [supplemented as necessary by 'Welfare Codes', standards and guidance], as required; see Section 16 (9).

Section 16 (3): Information which has to be kept available and has to be supplied for inspection.

Section 16 (4): This enables the authorities to know the location and contact details of all animal enterprises, so they can identify unauthorised activities; and/or advise enterprises of any new requirements or prohibitions.

Section 16 (7): When certain activities using animals are prohibited, the welfare needs of the animals should be prioritised when determining optimum transitional periods. For example, in the case of bans on circuses, a short transitional period may lead to animals' lives being taken needlessly, simply because it takes some time to successfully relocate wild animals. Whereas in other situations, such as farming situations where animals are suffering during their lifespan and are due to be killed shortly in any case, then a shorter transitional period would be preferable. Each situation should be determined on its merits, from the standpoint of animal welfare.

Section 16 (8): This provision will work to encourage keepers or producers of animals for business or economic activities to put pressure on their breeders to obtain the necessary authorisation for breeding, and thereby ensure that they are controlled by the competent authorities to ensure compliance with animal welfare requirements. It is a safeguard to protect the health and welfare of animals in the commercial supply chain.

Section 16 (9): Businesses with a high rate of unwanted animals, such as racing horses or greyhounds, should be carefully monitored and in case of any ongoing problems with surplus animals, such businesses or activities should be closed down, or at the very least only authorised if they fund shelters or sanctuaries for animals no longer used.

Section 16 (10): This provision authorises the Competent Authority to issue regulations [and, as appropriate, 'Welfare Codes', standards and guidance] covering any or all aspects of keeping or breeding animals in the scope of business or economic activities. These would include (but not be limited to)

- The power to withdraw or deny authorisations for any particular type of category of activity or any species of animal, or to restrict authorisation to stipulated species and numbers of animals (in the light of changing scientific research, needs or requirements, particular welfare concerns, or moral criteria). *[Thus ensuring that fresh authorisation would need to be obtained before any novel or different species were introduced, or any increase made to the numbers of animals - above the maximum authorised (which may affect animal welfare)]; and*
- Authority to issue detailed requirements concerning authorisation and application processes (including aspects such as record keeping; premises, facilities and accommodation; feeding and care; health and hygiene; skills/training; and humane methods for animal management activities); and even the implementation of a complete ban on the keeping of certain animal species or the production, possession, sale, offering for sale, or use of certain animal products. *[To ensure that international obligations can be met (for example, CITES restrictions); as well as ensuring that protection can be afforded to vulnerable animals including those whose conservation status or welfare needs are threatened].*

This will enable the authorities to follow the general principles established in Section 6 and, in particular,

Section 6 (4) (whereby the different purposes for which animals are kept and used must be regularly re-evaluated) and Section 6 (5) (whereby when it is found that the needs of different species cannot be met in captivity, the species must not be kept by humans).

Section 17   Sale and Trading of Animals

Section 17 (1): If the ownership of an animal is transferred to another person/enterprise it has to be ensured that the person/enterprise who will now be in charge of the animal has all the general knowledge and information to be able to care for the animal's well-being in all aspects. This provision deals with this need, and provides for evidence of compliance so the Competent Authority is able to enforce the provision.

Section 17 (2): This section is similar to Section 16 (1) but relates to the trading and sale of animals. It requires authorisation in accordance with Section 29. The list provided in Section 29 (1) is a non-exhaustive enumeration of activities which require authorisation from the authorities; and there should be discussion and consultation on which activities should be expressly included.

As has been stated in regard to Section 16 (1) above, this system provides a helpful framework for the authorities to establish and notify relevant requirements (with updates as necessary), and to carry out effective enforcement. These provisions will help to maintain permanent supervision and control on the trade of animals, which should serve to protect animals from unregulated breeding as well as from any unchecked black-market-type trading. However, the private transfer of ownership of individual animals within the regulations of the subject Act still can be undertaken without restrictions or any need for authorisation.

Sections 17 (3) - (9): The comments given under Section 16 (2) – (8) above apply, as relevant to the trading and selling of animals.

Section 17 (6): In some countries (such as the U.S.), this provision may evoke constitutional concerns, where no appeal rights are issued. This may not be the case elsewhere, but an effective appeals procedure is recommended in all cases, to avoid any unjust application of the provision.

Section 17 (10): This provision has been included to ensure that dogs and cats are not offered for sale at random sales outlets, as this would not only be detrimental to the welfare of the animals being held for sale, but could also encourage impulse buying (which frequently leads to later abandonment or neglect). Ideally other animals prone to spontaneous purchasing, such as rabbits, guinea pigs, hamsters etc., should also fall under this prohibition.

Section 17 (11): This provision specifically authorises the Competent Authority to restrict or ban the trade or sale of certain wild animals and/or wildlife products. This is to ensure that international obligations can be met (for example, CITES restrictions); as well as ensuring that protection can be afforded to vulnerable animals including those whose conservation status or welfare needs are threatened. Likewise in countries where the breeding and releasing of transgenic animals has been banned simultaneously the sale and trading of transgenic animals has to be prohibited, too.

This rule is separated from the general provision to introduce regulations [supplemented as necessary by 'Welfare Codes', standards and guidance] contained in Section 17 (12) for purposes of emphasis and expressed intent. This protection has to be read in conjunction with Section 16, which includes the power to introduce a complete ban on the keeping of certain animal species or the production, possession, sale, offering for sale, or use of certain animal products. The logic for this separation is that this section deals with trade and sale of animals; whereas Section 16 deals with the 'Keeping of Animals within the Scope of Business Activities'.

Section 17 (12): This would include the power to withdraw or deny authorisations for any particular type of trading or selling activity or any species of animal, or to restrict authorisation to stipulated species and numbers of animals (in the light of changing scientific research, needs or requirements, particular welfare concerns, or moral criteria); authority to issue detailed requirements concerning authorisation requirements and the application process (including aspects such as record keeping; premises, facilities and accommodation; feeding and care; health and hygiene; skills/training); and even the implementation of a complete ban on the trading or selling of certain animals or animal products as well as certain methods of selling – for example, a ban on the selling of animals over the Internet is highly recommended; and many countries ban the selling of companion animals through public sales or displays (in order to prevent impulse buying and protect their welfare).

This goes wider than wildlife alone, and may be needed to protect animals other than wildlife, in relation to any threat to their welfare or conservation status (and this protection also has to be read in conjunction with the Explanatory Notes of Section 16 (9)).

Section 18 Abandoned, Stray or Lost Animals and Confiscated Animals

These provisions would cover various species of animals, and need to be carefully drafted to take account of the local situation. For example, whilst stray dogs may need to be managed in some high population urban communities (to preserve animal and human health and welfare), in other places – such as rural areas or townships, stray dogs may be welcomed and cared for communally as 'community' animals. In some countries, farmed animals may also graze communally or wander (including, for example, cows and/or horses abandoned by their previous owners or keepers).

Section 18 (1): Within the law the Competent Authority has the duty to guarantee the proper accommodation and care of any abandoned, stray or lost animal, and equally for any animal which has been confiscated or taken away by the authority, or their designated agents.

The system established by the Competent Authority would need to determine who they would designate as agents for the capture, removal and taking away of these animals. Responsibilities would need to be delineated, and appropriate conditions agreed. In this regard, the usual choice is either for municipalities/local authorities to employ their own 'Animal Wardens' for this purpose or to contract the duty to appointed 'Animal Welfare Officers', who usually work for animal welfare organisations/animal shelters and have undergone appropriate training in the capture and handling of animals.

The OIE's international standard on Stray Dog Population Control states that the Veterinary Services should play a leading role in dog population management, coordinating their activities with other competent public institutions and/or agencies. The same principle should apply to other species.

The Police Service is also frequently required to play a part, usually in relation to enforcement.

The Competent Authority would also need to determine who they would accept as an appropriately authorised person, institution or organisation to house, care for – and possibly neuter and rehome – these animals. Here again, some municipalities/local authorities have their own animal holding facilities – and there is no objection to this, providing the welfare needs of the animals can be secured. However, contracting animal welfare organisations to carry out the duty is the most common option: This can help to provide a comprehensive and welfare-friendly service, whilst also using the animal welfare organisation and its contacts to promote re-homing of unwanted animals, and responsible animal care education and awareness.

In this case the animal shelter or institution would take over this obligation as an explicitly defined own mission.

Any animal shelter or institution being assigned this duty would need to comply with the legally stated prerequisites.

Section 18 (2): The animal shelter or institution should receive appropriate compensation for its services, and any related expenditure, from the authorities. The amount and form of remuneration would be agreed upon between the authorities and the animal shelter or institution. For example, a contract could be established setting out the concrete modalities, including set compensation for services in form of fixed daily fees, plus an agreement to refund any reasonable associated 'out of pocket' expenses.

The owner of the animal remains liable for repayment of all reasonable service charges and expenses incurred for the capture and safeguarding of the animal (as a civil debt) – provided he/she can be located.

Section 18 (7): This could include any necessary further provisions in the context of abandoned, stray or lost animals and confiscated animals. These could include

- The delineation of responsibilities, including a 'duty to enforce';
- Detailed requirements concerning the designation of agents for the capture, removal and taking away of these animals, including responsibilities, powers and appropriate terms and conditions (including aspects such as authorisation/licensing, skills/training, transport and equipment, record keeping, and access for inspection checks);
- Detailed requirements concerning the authorisation/licensing of persons, institutions or organisations to house, care for – and possibly neuter, vaccinate and rehome – these animals, including responsibilities, powers and appropriate terms and conditions (including aspects such as authorisation/licensing, skills/training, premises, transport and equipment, record keeping, and access for inspection checks);
- Procedures regarding the official publication of animals found; and
- Prerequisites and conditions when ownership can be transferred to a third party (for example, neutering and checks on potential new owners).

Section 19   General and Commercial Transport of Animals

The legal regulations on animal transport do not only cover the transport itself, which includes any kind of transfer or relocation of the animal from one place to another, but also the loading and unloading of the animal.

Section 19 (1) - (5): Are general provisions, covering all live animal transport. The remainder of the provisions cover only the commercial transport of live animals (carried out in connection with any business/economic activity).

Section 19 (6) Pt. 4: Space allowances will need to be determined based on latest scientific evidence and best practice. The European Food Safety Agency (EFSA) recommends in its 'Scientific Opinion Concerning the Welfare of Animals during Transport' (EFSA Journal 2011; 9(1)), (pp 81-84), a more flexible and objective approach for the establishment of space allowance (than the current tables based on species, and using large intervals). Animal transports involve all different age/weight stages, and EFSA considers that an allometric equation would give a much more objective calculation of the space allowance to the benefit of animal welfare and, at the same time, be of great assistance for both the transporters and the controlling authorities. They also recommended that space allowance for horses should be seen in relation to area per kg rather than area per animal. Space allowances also need to be adjusted for journey times and ambient climatic conditions.

Section 19 (2) and (6) Pt. 9: Feeding and watering requirements need to be appropriate to the method of transport, as well as the species and individual animal. For example, it may not be practical to use water containers on the floor, due to potential spillages and contamination, so nipple drinkers should be provided as an alternative. In such cases, animals may need to be acclimatised to drinking in a new way before they are transported (otherwise they can die of dehydration because they are unable to use the form of water dispenser available).
Another example would be the transportation of aquatic animals, where their welfare could be impaired by excretions in their water, if they were fed shortly before or during transport.

However, in the case that practical circumstances demand certain exemptions from general provisions, then species-specific requirements must be introduced in the form of regulations, 'Welfare Codes' or standards to protect the welfare of the animals during transport. Where this cannot be achieved consideration has to be given to introducing a complete ban on this life transport.

Section 19 (6) Pt. 13: The system of prior authorisation, based on the provision of route plans submitted in advance, is a vital part of enforcement. It necessitates prior planning on the part of the transporter, and enables the Competent Authority to arrange for veterinary inspection of 'fitness to travel' (and checks on other transport-related requirements). It can also link in with vehicle tracking and monitoring, to ensure that any maximum journey times, or staging and resting requirements, are correctly actioned. It is important that the veterinarian who is responsible for certifying 'fitness to travel' is responsible to the Competent Authority, as opposed to paid for by the transporter – to ensure fair and independent assessment.

To Pt. 16: The Competent Authority has to establish rules and regulations on ascertaining the individual animal's fitness for transport, set maximum journey times as well as regular rest intervals and feeding and watering times. It is recommended that longer journeys (over 8 hours) are banned entirely. As regards fitness to travel, detailed rules shall be produced to ensure that an animal must be fit for the intended journey before the journey starts and must remain sufficiently fit throughout the journey. This means the animal should be healthy enough to tolerate the entire journey it is about to make (including loading, unloading and any journey breaks) with no or very little adverse effect on it; the journey should not cause the animal any suffering or injury. The OIE Code sets out in detail the types of animals that are considered unfit to travel and in any case of doubt, the precautionary principle should be applied.

To Pt. 17: Provision has been made for a special license for international trade, transport and sea journeys. This enables closer supervision and control of these journeys (and also the establishment of additional safeguards or the withdrawal of categories of special licences/permits where welfare problems are encountered). In this case further requirements will need to be imposed (for example staging points, resting periods and extra feeding and watering provisions). CITES implementation may also require specific measures to protect certain species. Furthermore, consideration should be given to prohibiting the export of live animals, replacing this by trade in carcasses or meat products. This is important from two perspectives: both the avoidance of suffering during transport and the fact that a country is unable to regulate and control the treatment and killing of its animals outside its jurisdiction.

Each country will need to consider its approach, based on its own situation. For example, whilst it may appear to be in the interests of animal welfare to ban certain types of sea transport for live animals, in some island states, a sea journey may be the only way to deliver an animal to the nearest slaughterhouse.

Section 19 (7): These would include any detailed provisions and guidelines which have to be taken into account in this context of live animal transport, including

- The delineation of responsibilities, including a 'duty to enforce' and enforcement procedures and protocols to ensure effective and uniform enforcement;
- The means of transport: vessels, aeroplane, vehicle and container specifications (including fixtures and fittings, lighting, and ventilation/temperature control, stabilisation); and inspection and certification of the means of transport;
- Conditions and requirements for the registration and authorisation of businesses transporting animals;
- The training and certification of transporters, drivers and handlers of live animals;
- Additional specific requirements relating to the advance submission of journey plans and the authorisation system, including contingency plans for emergencies and requirements for journey tracking and logging;
- Detailed requirements for suitable facilities and equipment at the start and end of the journey, and at any stops for resting/staging points during the journey: for the assembly, loading, unloading and holding of animals; for the washing and disinfection of vehicles after unloading; for emergencies and veterinary inspections; and the humane killing of animals when necessary;
- The proper treatment of animals during transport and in loading and unloading: provision of adequate numbers of suitable trained and certified staff, particularly during loading and unloading; feeding, watering and rest requirements (including minimising any delays); inspection; veterinary assistance; temperature and humidity monitoring; protection from the elements; and the provision of appropriate bedding;
- Special provisions for veterinary supervision, disease control, preventative actions to minimise delays to live transport consignments, and emergency response measures;

- Specific requirements for different species, including detailed rules on fitness to travel (e.g. prohibitions on the transport of young animals (*with age recommendations for different species*), deer in velvet, shorn sheep in cold weather, or species in hot weather etc.); partitioning and mixing of animals; appropriate restraint, space and height allowances etc.;
- Any special requirements for animals transported by rail, road or sea, or over long distances;
- Provisions governing travelling times, and water, feed and rest – including the establishment of maximum journey times for the transport of live animals, particularly for journeys to slaughter; and
- Requirements for record keeping and powers of entry.

The latest animal welfare research should always be considered before establishing detailed requirements. For example, careful consideration should be given in relation to any requirements leading to journeys being broken (staging points for feeding or resting) – as unnecessary loading and unloading can exacerbate animal welfare problems unless sufficient time is given for recovery.

International requirements should also be taken into account – such as the International Air Transport Association's (IATA) regulations, CITES requirements, and the OIE's international animal welfare standards (transport of animals by land, sea and air; and the transport of farmed fish).

It is also important to note that the improper transport of an animal which leads to an animal's injury or to the animal suffering or experiencing pain, fear or distress can be penalised according to Section 7 AWA, i.e. 'Cruelty to Animals' (note Section 7 (2) Pt. 22). This would cover cases of inappropriate transport such as, for example, transporting an animal in the trunk of a car.

Section 20   Humane Killing and Slaughter of Animals

This section covers all humane killing and slaughter, regardless of species and method. This is to ensure the application of coherent animal welfare principles across the board. However, detailed requirements will need to be elaborated to cover individual species, as they have very different needs and requirements to achieve a humane death.

Without prejudice to the prohibition of killing animals according to Section 9 and notwithstanding Section 7, Section 20 now states that the killing of an animal is only allowed if it is ensured that it is carried out in a humane way (with care, circumspection, respect, and as little negative effect on the animal as possible). The prohibition in Section 9 relates to the killing of animals without any 'sound justification'. The production of food and other staple products is generally regarded as such a justification, (as would be, for example, the killing of animals for the purpose of 'pest' or disease control). However, as stated in the 2008 Policy of WSPA (now World Animal Protection), the different purposes for which animals are used must be regularly re-evaluated. For example, the killing of animals for inessential or luxury items (such as fur production or perfumes) could be viewed as 'unsound'.

One other vital aspect of Section 20 is that killing or slaughtering any animal without prior and effective anaesthetisation or stunning before death is absolutely prohibited (see sub-section (3), as well as sub-section (5)) except in the case of emergency killing/slaughter (according to sub-section (4), (*where general principles still apply*). This specifically excludes cases where the animal is killed instantaneously due to the fact that this can be the most humane way of ending an animal's life (because there is no possibility of the animal regaining consciousness in pain, as there is with stunning followed by exsanguination).

Regulations/detailed provisions on humane killing and slaughter should include all relevant requirements from the OIE's international standards, including slaughter of animals for human consumption and dog population management (which has a section on euthanasia).

Section 20 (2) and (5): The provision regarding veterinary assistants can be amended to suit the prevailing system, i.e. whether veterinary assistants are registered, certified or licensed (or indeed any other form of authorisation) to practice as such.

Section 20 (4): Detailed guidance provided on the killing of animals and farmed fish for disease control purposes likewise should incorporate the provisions of the OIE's international standards on these subjects.

Section 20 (7) and (12): A system of certification has been included for personnel as a means of ensuring that the necessary training has been undertaken, and the required degree of competence reached to safeguard animal welfare. This will enable the Competent Authority to accredit bodies to carry out the training, and to approve any training courses in advance. The requirement for certification will ensure that employers only recruit properly qualified staff, or assist personnel to train to the requisite level. The system can be amended and applied as suits local requirements e.g. licensing or registration, as opposed to certification.

Section 20 (8), (9) and (12): Detailed guidance issued on the design and construction of slaughterhouses should also include the principles given in the OIE's international standard on the slaughter of animals for human consumption. A system of licensing has been included so the Competent Authority can ensure that all new slaughterhouses are designed to meet the necessary requirements. This prevents the situation occurring when new facilities are constructed which do not meet the latest standards; and then the costs of dismantling prove exorbitant or prohibitive. A reasonable transition period can be given for existing facilities to be updated to compliant standards.

Section 20 (11): Some countries already prohibit ritual or religious slaughter, as this prolongs death and suffering. However, where religious slaughter is permitted for specified local religious communities, then there should be a provision requiring immediate post-cut stunning; or – preferably – simultaneous stunning and throat cutting. Where this is permitted, a system is recommended where prior authorisation is required to approve limited religious slaughter, providing there is the required simultaneous or post-cut stunning; and systems to ensure that the meat produced is only provided to the relevant local religious communities.

Section 20 (12): Such provisions would contain restrictions or even implementation of a complete ban on certain killing or slaughter practices (including methods of restraint, stunning/anaesthesia or killing) or detailed provisions and guidelines which have to be taken into account in this context of humane killing or slaughter of animals, including

- Requirements and specifications on the design and construction of slaughterhouses and lairages; their installations, equipment and instruments;
- Requirements for the licensing of slaughterhouses and their installations, equipment and instruments including transitional periods during which existing facilities, installations and systems may be sold and used; allocation of responsibilities for licensing; allocation of costs; and procedures for official inspections;
- The stunning, slaughtering and killing of animals, including the exsanguinations of animals;
- Requirements for different species of animal including: appropriate care and welfare, unloading, movement/handling, restraint, stunning and anaesthetisation, humane killing, slaughtering and exsanguination;
- The requirement to unload and lairage animals as soon as possible after arrival at a slaughterhouse;
- The unloading, movement and handling of animals to and in lairages and slaughterhouses, including appropriate use of animal behaviour;
- The requirement to slaughter/kill sick or injured animals humanely as soon as they arrive at the slaughterhouse (if possible at the site where they are found to be sick or injured, without being moved);
- The requirement to humanely slaughter/kill lactating animals as soon as possible after arrival at the slaughterhouse;
- The transportation and accommodation of animals within slaughterhouses;
- The restraint and containing of animals before anaesthetising, slaughtering or killing;
- Care and welfare of animals in the lairage and slaughterhouse;
- Any restrictions and special provisions covering ritual or religious slaughter, if permitted. Conditions for the establishment and authorisation of slaughterhouses dedicated to ritual/religious slaughter, measures to ensure that such meat is only consumed by the relevant religious community, and additional animal welfare safeguards for such slaughter methods where permitted;

- Restrictions on the substances/preparations which can be used for humane killing or anaesthesia, and guidance on the administration/use of permitted substances/preparations to ensure a humane death;
- Detailed provisions on the welfare of animals during killing for disease control;
- Special requirements for aquatic animals;
- The euthanasia of companion animals;
- The type of knowledge and skills required by staff, including training and expert knowledge, and details of the certification system for proof of compliance (including bodies accredited to conduct training and certification); and
- Requirements for record keeping and powers of entry.

Section 21   Principles of Animal Training

Section 21 (2): Animal trainers need to be registered by the Competent Authority in order to facilitate the notification of any particular protective provisions, and to enable appropriate enforcement inspections to be carried out. It is recommended that each country investigates its own position as regards such sports, performances and exhibitions before deciding how to approach this provision. If there are many, and many of these are small-scale, then it may be considered necessary to include a 'de minimus' provision (exempting small-scale non-commercial events from the requirement to register). However, it is recommended that all commercial events are required to be registered (and pay an appropriate registration fee). Also it is suggested that any animal welfare concerns about exempted sports, performances and exhibitions are carefully investigated, with a view to removing the exemption if they are found to adversely affect animal welfare.

Sections 21 (3) - (5): If there is any doubt that the training of certain species; use of substances and drugs; or the use of training devices, aids or tools could contravene the provisions of this Act or impair animal welfare, then they should be prohibited. The provision to restrict use should only be applied in cases where there are no foreseen adverse impacts on animal welfare (but where it is considered that such use should be controlled and monitored as a precautionary measure).

Section 21 (3): Careful consideration should be given to the types of animal training that will be permitted. For example, the Competent Authority may decide to prohibit all training of wild animals, because this would be contrary to their natural species-specific behaviour and/or because such training would be likely to impair the animal's welfare. But the Competent Authority might wish to consider permitting some degree of positive training of some wild animals where in the interest of the welfare of the individual animal (for example, to allow for safe handling for the purposes of veterinary inspection and/or treatment).

However, the Competent Authority may consider prohibiting all training (or indeed use) for itinerant animal shows in general because the transport and confinement inherent in this form of entertainment are likely to compromise animal welfare.

Section 21 (4): This provision requires the Competent Authority to bring forward measures to prohibit [or restrict] the use of any substances or drugs to enhance an animal's performance or modify its behaviour because such substances/drugs can impair animal welfare. For example, drugs can mask pain – which can have the effect of making an animal perform beyond its natural limitations and/or despite injury or damage.

Section 21 (5): This provision requires the Competent Authority to bring forward measures to prohibit [or restrict] the use of certain technical training devices, aids or tools which could impair animal welfare. It is recognised that not all training devices, aids or tools would be detrimental to animal welfare. However, some clearly are – such as those employing electric shocks, or otherwise designed to produce pain (such as whips, spike collars, coral type pronged collars etc.).

Section 21 (6): This provision seeks to prohibit any use of a live animal to train a dog or other animals in ways that affect the welfare of the animal or the dog or other animals. However, this does not rule out training a dog for herding or guarding.

Section 21 (7): Unannounced inspections are necessary, otherwise training methods cannot be effectively checked.

Section 21 (8): These would contain restrictions or detailed provisions and guidelines which have to be taken into account in this context of animal training, including

- Conditions and requirements for the registration and authorisation of persons and/or businesses training any animal for competitive or public sports, performance or exhibition.
- The type of knowledge and skills required by persons training animals for competitive or public sports, performance or exhibition, including details of bodies accredited to conduct such training. *[This could be included under the registration procedure envisaged in Section 21 (2) above. However, a distinct provision is recommended in case the Competent Authority decides to restrict registration to businesses, whilst introducing a separate system of skills accreditation/certification for each individual animal trainer. This provision also authorises the Competent Authority to appoint accredited training providers.]*
- Prohibitions and restrictions on the training of certain species of animals and/or the training of animals for certain types of sports, performance or exhibition.
- Detailed provisions on the welfare of animals during training.
- Listing prohibited technical devices, aids or tools for the training of animals for sports, performance or exhibition.
- Requirements for record keeping and powers of entry.

CHAPTER 4: SPECIFIC CATEGORIES OF ANIMAL USE

Section 22   Companion Animals (Pet Animals)

Section 22 (1): Education and awareness programmes shall be designed to deter impulse buying of companion animals, encourage spaying and neutering of dogs and cats, prevent straying, and ensure that keepers understand how to care for their animals in order to safeguard their health and welfare.

Section 22 (2): The Competent Authority must monitor companion animal ownership and any problems arising to ensure that management measures are introduced in a timely and effective manner. The form of registration and identification implemented should be effective and suitable for the country's socio-cultural environment and stage of technological development. For example, microchipping is an excellent technology for identification, but is only practical where equipment such as microchip readers can be rolled out nationally. In other cases, low tech solutions such as tattooing may be more practical.

Money from registration fees must be spent on animal welfare programmes for companion animals, including responsible ownership education and awareness.

Section 22 (3): Consideration should be given to making an annual visit to a veterinarian compulsory, either for an annual vaccination (where disease risk requires) or for an annual health check. However, this will need to be reviewed for each country individually, depending on criteria such as disease risk, animal health issues and availability and accessibility of veterinary services.

Section 22 (4): Free or low cost spay-neuter services may be an expensive endeavour initially, but on the other hand constitute an effective incentive for the owner to have their animals spayed/neutered and at the same time the decreases in the stray animal population that result will be favourable to any (developing) country. It will aid tourism to not have packs of roaming dogs on the streets, for instance. Collaboration with private sector veterinarians (e.g. in programmes to spay-neuter and vaccinate stray dogs) and NGOs (animal welfare organisations) is a common feature of dog management programmes. Indeed, the Competent Authority (or local authority) may invite tenders for companion animal stray management services, including animal warden/animal welfare officer services. In such cases, tenders and contracts must be carefully framed to ensure that the animals' welfare is protected.

Section 22 (6): Trap, Neuter, Release (TNR) programmes have been found to be an effective population control method for feral cats and dogs. They have also been used to control wild rabbit populations, and there has been interest in trialling programmes on other species (particularly introduced non-indigenous species). It is important that legislation is implemented to facilitate their use where they have been found to be effective and in the animals' welfare interests, ensuring that there are no legal barriers (e.g. no possibility of prosecution for capturing/releasing wild animals in such cases). However, work is ongoing to develop non-surgical neutering methods, and these may provide a more humane alternative (particularly for wild animals, where capture and handling can be stressful).

Section 22 (7) and (8): Some countries may decide to have an explicit prohibition on killing healthy animals, in which case these provisions will need to be amended accordingly. However, this may not be feasible in other countries, (for example, where there is a serious stray control problem and no extensive shelter network, or where spay/neuter-release for both dogs and cats is not considered acceptable). It is for each country to decide on an appropriate approach for its own circumstances.

Section 22 (9): The approach of producing a positive list of species that may be kept as companion animals is preferred to the prohibition of certain species. Such a list automatically prohibits all others, and thus is less likely to become outdated and inadequate. The assessment of which species should be covered on a positive list would include

- Animal welfare criteria;
- Degree of domestication;
- Adaptation to human contact/proximity;
- Risk of zoonotic disease;
- Risk of injury to humans; and
- Conservation aspects (e.g. risk of capture and depletion of wild populations).

There could be an initial list for mammals, followed by lists for reptiles and birds. Consideration would need to be given as to whether existing companion animals of other species would be registered and allowed to remain with their keeper whilst still alive, or confiscated (which may give rise to logistical and ethical issues).

Considerations in this regard are that wild or exotic animals, such as primates, reptiles, ornamental fish and wild birds are not suited to life in captivity. It is impossible to recreate the environment and climate to meet their needs in captivity. Also, most individuals have neither the finances nor the experience to care for them properly (and it has been estimated that 90% are dead within the first two years of captivity). Many wild animals forced into a domestic situation cause injury to humans, especially children. Others, if released into the environment, can cause irreversible and costly damage to the ecosystem.

Section 22 (10): These provisions could cover all areas of companion animal ownership and stray management. These would incorporate restrictions or detailed provisions, and guidelines for the prevention of companion animal problems, population control and stray dog management including

- The introduction of requirements for the enclosure of dogs and other companion animals, and leash laws for animals taken outside the home, in cases where there are animal welfare, health or safety concerns, such as in busy urban areas.
- The introduction of control measures for any dogs which may be dangerous to people or other animals. These shall not be breed-specific, and shall not be detrimental to animal welfare.
- The introduction of environmental controls to restrict available food sources (a recognised component of stray management). In particular, food sources which attract and maintain strays which can be found around abattoirs, rubbish dumps, dead stock facilities, restaurant and hotel yards etc.
- The allocation of duties and responsibilities to local authorities, including the establishment of a network of facilities for housing and re-homing stray companion animals, and the development of constructive working relations with animal welfare organisations.
- Detailed provisions on population control measures, including the aspects discussed in the notes in Section 22 (6) above.

To elaborate some of the above mentioned aspects in more detail:

There may for instance be a need for provisions concerning the enclosure of dogs and other companion animals within the home boudary in busy urban areas (where animals could be in danger if they stray and/or cause road traffic accidents). There may also be a need to introduce local leash laws, for similar reasons. However, the requirements of Section 12 (4) would also need to be taken into account in any such provisions.

The introduction of control measures for any dogs which may be dangerous to humans or other animals shall not be breed-specific, and should be carefully designed to ensure that such provisions are not more stringent than necessary, or detrimental to animal welfare. For example, legislation could make owners responsible for ensuring that any dogs which exhibit aggressive or potentially dangerous behaviour under any circumstances (however extreme) should be securely kept in the home enclosure and/or be muzzled at all times in public places. There could also be compulsory neutering, and a prohibition against breeding, for any dogs which have aggressive or potentially dangerous traits.

Breed-specific dog bans are to be avoided. For example, a country may not ban all pit bull terriers wholesale. There are several reasons for this: there is no hard and fast rule governing which breeds of dogs are dangerous and which are not; such a rule would make owning these dogs more palatable to people who should not own them, simply because they are forbidden; the rule would simply lead to the indoctrination of another breed as the 'rebellious' type of dog to own; and this rule would lead to the euthanasia of many dogs based solely on breed, and not on temperament.

Section 23   Animals Kept for Farming Purposes

Section 23 (1): The Competent Authority should publish minimum standards as guidelines to producers, importers and users of housing systems. Without such guidance, these businesses will find it difficult to assess potential compliance. However, as these standards only represent a bare minimum, and are likely to be improved and updated over time, businesses should be advised not to take these minimum standards as acceptable norms, but to produce, import and use higher-welfare systems.

Section 23 (3): The cost of this authorisation procedure shall be borne by the applicant. Housing systems and installations shall only be approved/licensed by the Competent Authority if all stipulated requirements are adhered to, and it can be demonstrated that such a system or installation will meet the welfare requirements of the animals. A condition to include CCTV in modern intensive systems is included to ensure that management and enforcement officers can effectively monitor and inspect the animals therein: The costs for this would be a small proportion of the overall cost of the system, and be far outweighed by the potential benefits.

Section 23 (4): There must be provision for an authorisation/license to be retroactively revoked if any of the particulars furnished in the application are subsequently found to be false; or if welfare problems become apparent in the ensuing use that could not be overcome by adjustments or alterations. In cases where scientific advances later prove that licensed systems are detrimentally impacting animal welfare, then it may be necessary to either compensate the business involved, or to permit a phase-in period for adjustments or system replacement.

Section 23 (6): In some very extensive systems it may not be feasible for animals to be inspected more frequently than once each day. However, in other cases it may be indicated to inspect more than once per day. In cases where more frequent inspections are required, these should be stipulated in regulations [and, as appropriate, 'Welfare Codes', standards and guidance].

Section 23 (8): This provision is considered desirable, based on the potential for animal suffering in cases of non-compliance. However, the feasibility of this will depend on the capacity of the veterinary services/competent authority.

Section 23 (9): It is important that any systems which are known to be inherently bad for animal welfare are listed and prohibited accordingly. In such cases, rules concerning the design, operation and use of alternative production systems should also be detailed. However, it may prove necessary to introduce phase-out periods in cases where significant investment and work is needed to change to more welfare-friendly systems. In all cases, phase-in periods should be kept to a minimum, and not subsequently extended, as animal welfare is compromised in the interim.

Section 23 (10): Prohibitions could be considered for (but not limited to) farming for fur, feathers, down and gourmet foods meeting these criteria.

Section 23 (11): Individual countries may have other farming practices which are detrimental to animal welfare and thus need to be prohibited in addition. In cases where the practices indicated are not currently used in a particular country, then it is recommended to introduce an immediate ban to prevent their introduction. This is necessary because these practices are increasingly being introduced and extended to countries where they are not traditionally used. Forced molting is a practice used by the commercial egg industry to induce a flock of hens to molt simultaneously, usually by withdrawing food (in order to prolong or spur egg laying).

Cases where calves have not been provided with a specified minimum daily ration of fibrous food have been used in veal production (particularly for the production of white veal), thus the need for a requirement for them to be fed fibre 'in sufficient quantity' for health, growth and vigour.

Section 23 (12): As with companion animals (Section 22 (8)), the approach of producing a positive list of species that may be kept for farming purposes is preferred to the prohibition of certain species. Such a list automatically prohibits all others, and thus is less likely to become outdated and inadequate. The assessment of which species should be included on a positive list would include

- Animal welfare criteria;
- Degree of domestication;
- Adaptation to human contact/proximity;
- Risk of zoonotic disease;
- Risk of injury to humans; and
- Conservation aspects (e.g. risk of capture and depletion of wild populations).

Particular consideration should be given to the introduction of non-domesticated species for farming purposes. The general rule should be that in any cases of doubt animal species should be excluded from the list of species that are permitted to be kept for farming purposes. Particular concerns are when animals cannot be handled and provided with the necessary care and veterinary attention; cannot be consistently killed humanely; where captivity causes stress and/or disruption of usual social interactions and species-specific behaviours; when captivity may adversely impact upon wild populations or ecosystems; or where they may be a health or safety risk to humans or other animals.

Section 23 (13): These would cover all aspects of the welfare of animals kept for farming purposes, and would incorporate restrictions, prohibitions, and detailed provisions and guidelines for the welfare of animals, including fish and birds, kept for farming purposes.

Farmed fish are often forgotten, but their welfare equally needs to be safeguarded. In particular, fish should not be confined in a way that exposes them to suffering. Factors such as stocking density, water quality and direction of flow should be regulated to protect the welfare of individual fish. The handling, transport and killing of farmed fish should comply with general humane principles. It should be prohibited for fish farms to allow anglers into farms to play the fish and then throw them back. It should also be prohibited to hang living fish up (e.g. from a stick, rope, angle etc. that has been threaded through the fish body) or to keep living fish out of water for periods that would compromise their welfare (e.g. prior to killing).

Section 24   Animals Used for Experimentation (including Science, Research, Testing and Education)

The subject of animal experimentation and of tests on live animals is a very sensitive and complex issue; and one which requires a variety of perspectives to be considered – ranging from scientific to ethical; and often involving a balance between competing interests. It is never easy to balance the animal's need for protection and safeguarding from pain, suffering and distress on the one hand, and humankind's perception of animal experiments being necessary for progress in certain fields of research on the other. However, there are now agreed international principles governing animal experimentation, including an OIE international standard on 'The Use of Animals in Research and Education'. There is also a growing consensus that it is not just or ethical to use animals for purposes which are not vitally important to humans, animals or the environment.

In this Act, preference has been given to the inclusion of some of the most important fundamental provisions into the Animal Welfare Act itself, together with a controlling framework based on best practice. This will enable the Competent Authority to control and monitor animal experimentation, and the breeding of animals for experimentation, on its territory, whilst preparing to introduce detailed regulations [supplemented as necessary by 'Welfare Codes', standards and guidance].

Far more detailed requirements will need to be elaborated in supporting regulations [and, as appropriate, 'Welfare Codes', standards and guidance]. There is much useful information in the OIE's International Standard. There are also many detailed regulations from other countries and the EU that could serve as guidance in this regard. However, these will need to be relevant to the country and its own situation.

In some countries, animal experimentation is not seen to be a pressing animal welfare concern, simply because it is not widely practiced. However, experience has shown that animal experimentation can move from highly regulated environments towards non-regulated or lower-regulated, low-cost countries. Thus, it is vital to establish these controls before there has been industry development (possibly with investment in facilities, installations and systems which are detrimental to animal welfare).

Prominence has been given to the internationally accepted 3Rs (see Section 24 (5) as well as Section 6 (3) 2.). However, these need to be applied stringently and systematically in order to be effective. In particular, there is a hierarchy of application, whereby replacement should be the aim; followed by reduction where this has not been considered feasible; and refinement always applied to any animal experiments (refinement having a multi-faceted approach designed to minimise impacts on animal welfare).

The 3Rs principle should also be fully taken into account in the authorisation and ethical review processes for animal experiments. In particular, no authorisation should be given where alternative methods are available or where the use in question cannot be fully justified. The use of alternatives and prohibitions in other countries should be studied and taken into account before a decision is taken, and every effort made to ensure the early national adoption of all alternatives to prevent unnecessary animal use. (For example, the use of animals for medical training: As, for instance, trauma training which is not considered necessary or ethical, as human-based model simulators can be used (and are in some countries).

Section 24 (3): The Competent Authority should consider requiring the application to be accompanied by a redacted copy for publication by the Competent Authority, identical in content except for the elimination of personal information, locations or commercially confidential information. This approach facilitates publication of experiment licences after the usual Freedom of Information measures (whilst protecting individual and organisational identities and commercially sensitive information).

Section 24 (18): This provision would cover educational uses such as the keeping of animals as school 'pets', and the use of animals for school demonstrations and educational visits. Whilst such uses are well-meaning, they might have a poor educational impact, whilst compromising the animals' welfare. There are particular problems during school holidays, when classroom 'pets' are taken home by pupils (who can quickly lose interest), and their welfare can no longer be overseen by staff.

Section 24 (19): The detailed rules and regulations governing animal experimentation. These shall include, but not be restricted to

- Conditions, requirements and procedures for the authorisation of animal experiments and granting of personal and project licenses; the licensing of breeding centres for experimental animals; and the licensing of premises where animal experimentation may be conducted. A licensing system has been used as this is common for controlling animal experimentation, but it is possible to amend this to another form of authorisation, such as certification or registration, if this is appropriate to the system prevailing in the jurisdiction.

- Detailed requirements for the ethical and scientific review of animal experiments before authorisation is granted. Ethical and scientific review shall be carried out locally (at the authorised premises) before an application for authorisation is submitted, and include: analysis of the need for the experiment, its scientific premise and soundness, ethical aspects, animal welfare impact, and whether it could entail duplication. After submission, it shall be thoroughly examined by the Animal Experimentation Sub-Committee referred to in Article 35 (4), which may call upon additional expertise and advice as necessary.
- Minimum standards for the premises where animal experiments may be conducted, including: animal facilities and accommodation; installations; equipment; inspection systems; and other systems used in carrying out experiments on animals.
- Minimum standards for facilities where experimental animals may be bred, including: animal facilities and accommodation; installations; equipment; and inspection systems.
- Detailed requirements for the accommodation, care and supervision of animals bred or used for experimentation, including: animal welfare and veterinary care (including pain management; anaesthesia and analgesia; and humane endpoints); housing; environmental enrichment; exercise and social interaction.
- Detailed requirements on qualifications, training and responsibilities for the named person responsible for experiments; the veterinary supervisor; and any other roles relating to the care and supervision of animals bred or used for experimentation.

In addition to those rules and regulations regarding animal experimentation itself, further provisions should be implemented to prohibit the funding and/or commissioning of research to be carried out in other countries where it would be prohibited by this Act.

Section 25 Wildlife and Animals Kept in Zoos/Aquaria

Historically, legal regimes dealing with wildlife have been associated with particular socio-economic structures (particularly land-owning classes seeking to create and protect rights over the wildlife present on their land). Wildlife was treated by the law as an economic or leisure resource, or as something to be controlled, rather than something worthy of protection in its own right. Animal welfare was hardly a consideration in these times, and most protective provisions were designed to protect endangered species – although there were some minor provisions aimed at curtailing the worst excesses of cruelty (for example, provisions such as a requirement to kill severely injured animals; and prohibitions such as shooting an animal from an aircraft, vehicle or mechanically propelled craft).

The utilitarian status of wildlife within the legislative regime began to change towards the latter half of the nineteenth century. However, wildlife welfare still needs to be given greater consideration; particularly to take better account of the sentiency of wildlife and the responsibilities of humans to captive wildlife.

It is important that legislation protecting the welfare of wild animals reflects and is consistent with general animal welfare principles. However, the special circumstances pertaining to wildlife (both in nature and in captivity) will naturally need to be considered, and the optimum approach taken for their welfare. Thus, this Act has focused on the approach that wild animals living in the wild with no 'owner' should be guaranteed a life as undisturbed as possible in their natural habitat, with optimal freedom. A similar principle should ideally be applied also to wild animals in protected areas.

As stated in the preamble to the Bern Convention (Convention on the Conservation of European Wildlife and Natural Habitats): "Wild flora and fauna constitute a natural heritage of aesthetic, scientific, cultural, recreational, economic and intrinsic value that needs to be preserved and handed on to future generations." Wildlife is part of a valuable biodiversity and natural heritage which needs to be protected. Wild animals are also fellow sentient animals. Thus, there is a human obligation to ensure that they do not suffer or perish at the hands of humans (or through human activity).

However, there is now very little wilderness area left, so the creation and development of protected areas is encouraged.

Nevertheless, some countries do still permit hunting in nature and/or in protected areas. If this is the case, then additional controls will be needed to protect the welfare of the animals (as well as the usual conservation controls, which are designed to protect species and numbers of animals, rather than the welfare of individual animals). These would include aspects such as: prohibition on hunting during mating and breeding and rearing seasons (not just for reasons of stock replenishment, but also for welfare reasons such as social hierarchies, family units, care of young wildlife etc.). The provisions on hunting proficiency certificates and prohibition of cruel killing methods are included as additional welfare safeguards.

Section 25 (1) and (2): Human activities, development and expansion are affecting wildlife habitats (their climate) and their welfare – and these side-effects of human activity are frequently not recognised until it is too late for the animals. Thus a system of animal welfare impact assessment is recommended (as is already used for environmental impacts, and for animal welfare in the EU) to forewarn and permit preventative action. Habitat encroachment can include wildlife corridors, buffer zones and migratory routes. Human activities can include use of chemicals, such as fertilizers and pesticides, which can impact wildlife adversely.

Each country should determine its own minimum standards for these animal welfare impact assessments, using available 'best practice'. Capacity building will be needed to ensure that these assessments are carried out effectively and in regular intervals; and wildlife rangers will need to be trained in animal welfare to ensure that they can guard against animal welfare infringements in the wild or protected areas.

Section 25 (4): As regards population control measures, non-lethal measures such as fertility control are continually being developed and refined. These should always be used where feasible, as opposed to lethal control measures.

Section 25 (7): Legal provisions may ban the keeping of some species of animals (negative or black list) or only allow some species to be kept (positive or white list). As this is a model law, a positive list system has been adopted. Whilst the negative list is the most commonly used system to regulate the keeping of wild animals, the use of positive lists is gaining support, as this is the most precautionary approach. On a negative list system, the default is that any animal not on a negative list is allowed to be kept, requiring the list to be quite long to ensure that animals with welfare, health, invasive or conservation risks are not kept. In addition it might not be adequate to address emerging trends and threats from the keeping of new exotic animals. Indeed, the process to add new species to the list is often slow and burdensome and the content of the list will thus lag behind the latest trends in the trade and keeping of exotic animals.

The objectively assessed criteria for listing or de-listing should include

- Animal welfare;
- Risk of zoonotic disease;
- Risk of injury to humans; and
- Pet exaptation (the ability to live in close proximity to humans).

A review of the positive list is intended to remove any species from the list where scientific advances or practical experience has shown that these cannot be kept without welfare problems. Great caution should be exercised in adding any species to this white list that have not previously been kept in captivity. This should only be done in case of a proven need, i.e. in cases where it is considered necessary for animal/human survival and where it can be proven beyond any reasonable doubt that the welfare needs of the animals can indeed be met in captivity. Keeping can also require authorisation in the form of a license.

Section 25 (8) and (9): A system of licensing has been suggested for hunting premises. However, it is possible to amend this to another form of authorisation (e.g. registration or certification), if appropriate to the system of the jurisdiction.

Section 25 (8) & (15): In no case should authorisation be given to any 'canned hunting' operations, as these are considered both unethical and detrimental to animal welfare. Ideally, all forms of non-conservation culling/hunting should be prohibited.

Section 25 (9): It is considered prudent to deny hunting licenses to individuals who are likely to pose a risk to animal welfare (for example, through demonstrated lack of concern for the welfare of animals, or general tendencies towards violent or aggressive behaviour). However, this has been restricted to any person who has been convicted (for violating any animal protection provision, or for any act of violence or aggression against humans) in order to ensure that there is proof in terms of prior conviction. Countries may also decide to introduce administrative measures to protect against potential human rights violations, by giving an individual the opportunity to prove that he or she is entitled and deserving of a certificate despite any prior conviction. If this approach is adopted, such procedures will need to be carried out vigilantly to prevent any potential risks to animal welfare.

Section 25 (10), (11) and (12): Hunting using inhumane methods should not be permitted. Every country will need to consider the methods which are currently being used, and introduce specific bans on any which are found to be inhumane (or, using the precautionary principle, where any doubt remains as to whether they are humane).

Section 25 (12): Certain methods known to be inhumane are prohibited from the outset. In other cases, the Animal Welfare Committee shall review methods of capture, entrapment and killing of animal, following which they will present a list of prohibited methods. In these cases, there will be a ban not only on their use, but also on the sale, offering for sale, advertising, import and export of unauthorised catching, trapping or killing devices and poisons.

Section 25 (15): A ban on such uses is strongly recommended because they cannot justify the inevitable welfare compromises. Should governments take a decision to permit any of these uses, then they should establish a system of licensing, with effective enforcement and monitoring, in order to regularly review and re-evaluate such uses.

Section 25 (16): Where wild animals are causing problems for local communities (e.g. those living adjacent to nature or protected areas), work should first be carried out together with local communities to try to mediate a solution – including education and awareness, and the development of targeted compensation schemes. There are also other cases, which involve wild animals moving into human domain, but which are commonly dealt with through 'pest control' measures (sometimes home solutions, and sometimes through 'pest control' professionals). We do not consider the term 'pest control' to be an appropriate or desirable descriptor, as it is often human activities that are problematic, as opposed to the animals. However, as this is common terminology, we have used it for avoidance of doubt, but placed it in quotation marks. We also consider that animal welfare principles should be applied consistently, regardless of whether such animals are considered a nuisance from a human perspective. A system of licensing has been suggested for 'pest control' businesses. However, it is possible to amend this to another form of authorisation (e.g. registration or certification), if appropriate to the system of the jurisdiction.

Section 25 (17): It should be noted that Education and Entertainment are not considered proven benefits for the purpose of this Act.

Section 25 (19): The conservation value of many zoological gardens (zoos and aquaria) is now being questioned, as the most valuable conservation programmes are carried out in situ. Breeding programmes only contribute to conservation efforts if the animals bred can be successfully reintroduced into sustainable natural wildlife habitats. The educational value of many zoos has also been questioned, as education based on captive wild animals which cannot live their lives free from human interference and compromised welfare is not considered positive. The welfare of many animals in zoos and aquaria is impaired due to factors such as: unsuitable enclosures, management practices, and social groupings. Therefore, great care and consideration should be given to the authorisation of any new zoos/aquaria. Where a decision is taken not to authorise an existing zoo, or to rescind the authorisation for an existing zoo/aquaria, then a period of grace may need to be given in order to rehome the remaining animals or to upgrade their facilities and care. Every effort should be made to ensure that displaced animals are humanely rehomed.

Section 25 (23): These could include any measures in the context of wildlife and zoos/aquaria, and include aspects such as

- Establishing the system and requirements for animal welfare impact assessments;
- The prerequisites and minimum requirements for the keeping of wild animals in captivity, taking into consideration both the objectives and other provisions of the subject Act, as well as the recognised state of scientific knowledge;
- Rules and conditions covering the keeping of wild animals in captivity;
- Special conditions and requirements for the application for, and issue of, hunting licenses;
- Special conditions and requirements for the application for, and issue of, hunting proficiency certificates and advanced hunting proficiency certificates; including eligibility criteria;
- Conditions and requirements concerning the advertising, naming and branding of any premises and businesses keeping wild animals to ensure that customers, tourists and the public are not misled about the nature of the business or their credentials;
- Requirements for record keeping and powers of entry and access to records;
- Prohibitions, limitations and controls on the trade in wild animals and their body parts or derived products; including prohibitions on the export of live wild animals for purposes other than over-riding animal welfare reasons; and
- Deterring and punishing such offences as illegal hunting, illegal trafficking, illegal trade, illegal possession, illegal processing and illegal consumption. In particular, specific provisions against reckless commission, to ensure that particular problems are identified and individuals made aware of the possibility of potential adverse consequences arising from their actions.

As regards 'reckless commission', requisite measures may include prohibiting

- All forms of deliberate capture or killing of wild animals (or specified species of wild animals) in the wild or protected areas;
- Deliberate disturbance of these species, particularly during the period of breeding, rearing, hibernation and migration;
- Deliberate destruction or taking of eggs from the wild; and
- Deterioration or destruction of breeding sites or resting places.

However, there will likely be other cases of 'reckless commission' in each country, which necessitate specific mention.

Wildlife conservation and hunting laws will need to be reviewed to ensure consistency with the agreed animal welfare principles.
In addition, it is important that a country makes use of ancillary legislation dealing with finance, money laundering and tax, to deter/punish those who attempt to benefit from the proceeds of wildlife crime.

Section 26   Animals Used for Work

It will be a requirement for a business using animals for working purposes to obtain authorisation in accordance with Section 16 andSection 29 of the Act. However, some jurisdictions may wish to impose a 'de minimus' on this provision (for example, restricting it to a minimum number of animals used), in order to make it less burdensome administratively and exempt individuals using their animal for subsistence income generation from the need to obtain authorisation. This would in no way exempt such animal users from compliance with the provisions of this Act.

Section 26 (4): Adequate shade or shelter will depend on the climate and any available natural shade and shelter.

In warm weather, measures to prevent heat stress would include: shady resting places, free access to drinking water, pouring water over animals (where appropriate), less work and more frequent resting periods. Where the weather is such that animals cannot be worked without discomfort or welfare problems, then they should not be worked at such times or under those specific conditions. Heat stress could be defined or cross-referenced with the OIE Chapter on Working Equids.

Section 27   Animals Used for Sports, Leisure and Entertainment

These provisions should be considered in terms of the fact that the use of animals for sports, leisure and entertainment can create significant human and animal welfare problems; as well as conservation problems in the case of wild animals. There can also be significant public safety issues surrounding the use of wild animals (including to animal trainers, children, and the public at large). The industry covers an enormous range of uses of animals and is probably also the least 'justifiable' form of animal use. These also have a negative educational impact on children, as regards respect and protection of sentient beings. Thus there are serious ethical and welfare considerations in this category of animal use.

This category of animal use also incorporates welfare considerations in respect of training (Section 21); keeping (Sections 12 and 13); disposal of animals when they are no longer able to perform (Sections 9, 10 and 20); and – in the case of itinerant sports, leisure or entertainments – transport (Section 19). As regards training, the techniques, devices, or agents used to make the animals perform are many times abusive, cruel, or stressful; causing suffering to the animals and creating a greater threat to the public.

Many of the associated welfare problems are not evident in the performance/event itself, which is the reason why welfare monitoring is suggested (for example, the disposal of animals no longer able to perform has been found to be a significant problem).

Section 27 (1) and (2): Careful consideration should be given to how best to enact this (and subsequent) provisions. Much will depend on the existing situation in the country, necessitating research and analysis. For example, some countries have a strong culture of animal use in entertainment, whereas others (particularly countries with their own wildlife populations in the wild, or nature reserves) have not taken this route. In general, the precautionary principle is advised, with uses being prohibited where it cannot be proven that the welfare needs of the animals can be secured – particularly given the fact that this use is not for purposes more essential than human entertainment.

Section 27 (3): The use of wild animals in such businesses involves significant welfare and conservation problems (for example, itinerant circuses cannot provide for the physiological and behavioural needs of wild animals, and have been involved in wildlife trade infringements). Many forward-looking countries thus prohibit the use of wild animals in this way. [For example, bans and phasing out of circuses and dolphinaria are increasingly common.] Others prohibit the introduction of any new businesses, and closely regulate and monitor existing ones.

Section 27 (7): A prohibition against bullfights and rodeos is recommended even in cases where such events do not take place in a country – as problems have occurred when promoters try to stage such events in different countries, and countries find they do not have the legislative backing required to prevent this from happening.

Section 27 (8): There are various systems and guidelines covering the use of animals in filming.

Section 27 (10): This provision will enable prohibitions or regulations to be extended in the event of new evidence or societal/ethical considerations. In some cases, new forms of animal entertainment may be devised, which would best be prohibited before they can gain popularity. Even some common uses of animals for sports, leisure and entertainment can be found to cause unacceptable welfare problems (for example, certain horse races – such as 'steeplechases' – where jumps are raised to a level that causes falls, injuries and deaths). In some countries, dog racing is prohibited, due to ethical/societal concerns as well as welfare problems.

Section 27 (11): These could include any prohibitions, restrictions or detailed provisions and guidelines in the context of animals used for sports, leisure and entertainment, including

- The prerequisites and minimum requirements for the use of animals in sports, leisure and entertainment, taking into consideration both the objectives and other provisions of the subject Act, as well as the recognised state of scientific knowledge;
- Rules and conditions covering the use of animals for film, still photographs, video or television productions;
- Special conditions and requirements for the authorisation of persons or businesses using animals for sports, leisure or entertainment;
- Conditions and requirements concerning the advertising, naming and branding of such persons or businesses to ensure consumers are not misled about the nature of their business or their credentials; and
- Requirements for record keeping and powers of entry.

As regards the advertising, naming and branding of such persons or businesses, some mislead consumers – for example, in the case of tourist wildlife menageries masquerading as 'sanctuaries' or 'zoos'/aquaria, when they have no genuine rescue or conservation programmes. Facilities which breed wild animals simply to attract visitors (for example, permitting close contact, 'petting' and stroking) can be unscrupulous in disposing of unwanted animals when they grow – and misinformed visitors think they are witnessing a conservation breeding programme.

Where itinerant acts are permitted, a notification system similar to that for animal transport should be considered, to enable unannounced spot-check inspections to be carried out. This would need to include a journey and exhibition/performance timetable, with detailed travel plans and venues, as well as details of the animals to be transported and the arrangement made for their care and welfare.

CHAPTER 5: IMPLEMENTATION AND ENFORCEMENT PROVISIONS

Section 28   Authorities

Section 28 (1): The relevant Ministry at central government level should be given overall responsibility for the policy and administration of this Act. This will enable it to co-ordinate all enforcement role players; and to provide overall responsibility for the mandate. There is discussion/advice about the decision on where to site the mandate above in IV. Proposed New Measures for Consideration, Competent Authority.

Section 28 (2): This provision enables the Competent Authority to use the expertise of the Veterinary Services in drafting or co-ordinating regulations [supplemented as necessary by 'Welfare Codes, standards and guidance'] or instructions and guidance of a technical nature. This is to ensure the full use of their expertise; but is in no way meant to over-ride the need to fully involve the Animal Welfare Committee, and to take account of its advice.

Section 28 (3): If the humane ethic is to be instilled in all areas where humans have dealings with animals, then animal welfare inspection and education should be made a duty for all authorities dealing with animals, as well as being a police matter.
This provision introduces a 'duty to enforce' the Act and any secondary legislation made under it for all relevant government bodies. It is recognised that some of these bodies will need to build expertise in animal welfare matters; and this capacity building will be the responsibility of the Competent Authority. However, targeted enforcement instructions and guidance notes (for specific areas of animal use/activity) will assist in this process.

Section 28 (4): The organs of public security/police officers have a clear duty to enforce this Act. This means that they will need to proactively include this in their functions and duties, rather than solely acting on the direct request of the Competent Authority. As with (3) above, it is recognised that organs of the public security/police will need to build expertise in animal welfare matters; and this capacity building will be the responsibility of the Competent Authority.

Section 28 (5): This provision provides a duty to enforce for lower tiers of government (for municipalities and, where appropriate, for regional governments – such as provinces or states). This is for the avoidance of doubt – e.g. to avoid any cases where regional or local government denies any mandate or responsibility for animal welfare, because this is deemed to be for the Competent Authority.

Section 28 (7): This provision enables the Competent Authority to appoint additional Animal Welfare Inspectors. This has proven to be a useful adjunct to enforcement by officials in cases where countries find themselves lacking in enforcement ability or resources. The most usual source of these additional Animal Welfare Inspectors is from within animal welfare organisations (where much of the animal welfare expertise resides). However, the optimum situation is when resources are made available for comprehensive official supervision; with additional checks permitted by representatives from animal welfare organisations.

In all cases where Animal Welfare Inspectors are appointed, they need to be granted the powers necessary to carry out the task, backed up by official identification and warrants.

Section 28 (8): A system of training and examination/interview will have to be established by the Competent Authority to ensure that only adequately trained and experienced professionals – with appropriate personal qualities and motivations – are granted a license to act as Animal Welfare Inspectors. A system of licensing has been suggested for Animal Welfare Inspectors. However, it is possible to amend this to another form of authorisation (e.g. registration or certification), if appropriate to the system of the jurisdiction.

Section 28 (9): The Competent Authority has the duty to monitor and enforce the proper compliance with the subject Act and all administrative decisions based on it. To meet this obligation the authority has the responsibility to ensure that competent officers/Animal Welfare Inspectors for the execution of this Act are engaged (of sufficient number to ensure regular and systematic monitoring). All of these officers/Animal Welfare Inspectors – whether from central or local government, or additional Animal Welfare Inspectors recruited from outside government – should not only possess the necessary professional qualifications, expertise and technical skills but also the desirable personal commitment and qualities (including compassion and empathy). An important part of the remit of these officers/Animal Welfare Inspectors will lie in areas which prevent animal welfare problems, such as: education, information and advice, particularly as concerns proper animal keeping and care. There will also be an imperative for the oversight of enforcement and inspection activities to ensure the quantity and quality of inspections. This should include a reporting system and inspection audits.

Section 29   Authorisations

As was explained in Part 1, IV. Proposed New Measures for Consideration, Content of the Law, this Act is only intended as framework legislation, establishing broad principles. The Act then authorises the Minister responsible, the Ministry or the Competent Authority to adopt any regulations [and establish, as appropriate, 'Welfare Codes', standards and guidance] needed to elaborate the concrete details for the implementation of these principles. This accords with the right and proper delineation between Parliament's governance function and Government's responsibility for implementation (avoiding a lengthy and over-technical Act for Parliamentary consideration, and facilitating subsequent amendments by the Executive based on experience gained and advancing scientific knowledge and the changing values and expectations of society).

A modern Animal Welfare Act lays down certain fundamental provisions to ensure the well-being of the individual animal. Where these cannot be met in certain areas of animal use, then prohibitions can be included in the Act. However, in other areas, concerns may exist over the ability to protect the welfare of animals, but there is not yet a consensus in favour of a prohibition. In these cases, a system of authorisation (based on licensing) can provide a framework which

- Can prevent the expansion of types of animal use and systems which are suspected of adversely affecting animal welfare;
- Provides a scheme for elaborating and notifying detailed requirements designed to protect the welfare of animals;
- Enables such requirements to be specifically tailored to each use and system (such as a zoo/aquaria, animal shelter, wildlife rehabilitation centre, breeding establishment, pet shop, farm, slaughterhouse etc.), and each species (i.e. housing and care of animals based on species-specific needs);
- Enables the elaboration of detailed requirements covering the professional, technical and personal skills and experience of persons working in these areas;
- Raises knowledge and awareness of animal owners, keepers and users;
- Puts animal owners, keepers and users on notice, given the possibility of losing their licence or even

ownership for certain infringements;

- Enables and facilitates the elaboration of provisions on enforcement, such as: inspections, powers of entry, access to animal keeping facilities, record keeping and reporting requirements; and
- Provides a feed-back and reporting system, which will facilitate regular review and reappraisal (in some cases leading to subsequent prohibitions; and in others to tightened requirements and enhanced enforcement).

This approach equates with the legal concept of 'proportionality', whereby the least onerous measures should always be adopted (when faced with a choice of approaches).

The list provided in Section 29 (1) is a non-exhaustive enumeration of activities which are subject to approval from the authorities; but there should be comprehensive discussion and consultation on which of these activities should be included in each country. Indeed, some countries would have different types of activities which need to be covered, so this can only be considered on a country-by-country basis. In such deliberations, prominence should be given to the inclusion of areas where exploitation and abuse is more likely to warrant additional protection. Authorisation should also be required where surveillance or monitoring is deemed necessary (for example, to determine whether any use has to be prohibited). In general, the aim should be to cover as many activities of keeping or breeding animals as possible, because the authorisation system provides a helpful framework for the authorities to establish and notify relevant requirements (with regular updates as needed), and to carry out effective enforcement.

Where the authorisation system or other feedback identifies a specific animal welfare problem which needs to be dealt with, consideration would have to be given as to whether this could be tackled though administrative procedures (for example, connected to the authorisation system), through the introduction of new implementing regulations [supplemented as necessary by 'Welfare Codes', standards and guidance], or through a combination of the two.

For example, in the case of a stray dog control problem

1. *The introduction of a compulsory dog license scheme (when overpopulation and straying become a real problem);*
2. *Measures to promote neutering (such as a graded rate of dog license fee, depending on whether a dog has been neutered or not);*
3. *Compulsory marking/identification of dogs (and cats) for the purpose of enforcement, and repatriating runaway animals;*
4. *Compulsory vaccination for problematic and prevalent diseases; and*
5. *Control over breeders and traders of companion animals/dogs.*

To some extent, countries may decide that they are unable to cope with the administrative requirements for an extensive system of authorisations. This would be regrettable, for the reasons given above. In such cases, it is strongly recommended that an authorisation system is at least brought into effect for the areas of animal use with the highest welfare problems or the lowest level of ethical justification. Thus the system can be trialled, inspections carried out, and an informed decision taken as to whether to prohibit the uses in question. Then, once the Competent Authority is familiar with an authorisation system and able to administer this effectively, it is hoped that it could subsequently be extended to other areas of animal use.

Consideration could be given to levying a licensing fee for the authorisation of any commercial establishment or activity using animals (breeding, keeping, using, transporting or trading), which should then be considered an animal welfare tax and retained in the budget for animal welfare activities. No fees/animal welfare taxes should be levied for non-profit and voluntary activities for the benefit of animal welfare.

Section 30   Nature of Enforcement

The Competent Authority will need to design an enforcement programme, based on a combination of these approaches. The aim should be to maximise the use of current supervision activities involving animals, by always including animal welfare inspections in these. For other activities involving animals, a proactive enforcement regime will need to be determined. In general, more resources should be directed towards prevention work and areas where there are prohibitions or controls (for example, authorisation requirements), as these have been implemented for good reasons.

Section 31   Powers of Enforcement Bodies

These powers shall be granted to all enforcement bodies, including appointed Animal Welfare Inspectors. This enables these officers to fulfil their enforcement duties effectively. However, the granting of such powers underlines the importance of authorising only competent and suitable professionals.

Section 31 (1): The bodies responsible for enforcement have the right to enter and inspect any premises or means of transportation regardless of whether this is in relation to a commercial animal keeping/use activity or in relation to private animal keeping. This is especially the case when there is suspicion of an infringement of this Act.

Section 31 (4): Wide-ranging powers are suggested to facilitate effective enforcement. However, these will need to be checked locally, as in some jurisdictions reasonable notice or a court order may be constitutionally required absent exigent circumstances. Also, consideration may be given to restricting power of access to private dwellings, possibly requiring a court order to enter in cases where there is reason to suspect a breach of the subject Act or any legislation made under it.
Where veterinary support is needed, the Competent Authority should have a list of authorised veterinarians with relevant skills and experience, including species-specific experts.

Section 31 (5): The provisions of Section 18 (1) and (2) with regard to lost, abandoned or confiscated animals apply accordingly to an animal which has been relieved or seized from its owner/keeper as per this Section.

Section 32   Improvement Notices

In more advanced animal welfare legislation, emphasis is given to the role of education and awareness in enforcement. An important part of an Animal Welfare Inspector's job is to generate awareness and to inform the public about proper animal keeping and care. Thus, the preference is for prevention (wherever feasible), as opposed to focussing on sanctions and punishments. This idea is at the core of this measure of an improvement notice.

Improvement notices can be given at the discretion of the enforcement officer/Animal Welfare Inspector in cases where he/she feels that an educational approach is appropriate. This action is recommended in cases where any omission or contravention has been carried out through lack of knowledge or awareness (rather than intentionally), and the enforcement officer/Animal Welfare Inspector feels that there will be no recurrence. However, it should be left to the judgement of the individual enforcement officer/Animal Welfare Inspector whether to issue an improvement notice or to implement prosecution proceedings without any further delay.

Therefore the Animal Welfare Inspector has the option to grant a culprit a period of grace in which to rectify the problem, remedy the defects, and comply with the provisions of the Act.

Improvement notices can be used for defects found to vehicles transporting animals and animal keeping systems, as well as for aspects of animal care.

Section 33 Duty to Alert and Report Offences and Duty to File a Criminal Complaint

Section 33 (1): This regulation is addressed to 'anybody', and thus provides a duty for all people (whether working with animals or not, including the general public) to report any suspicions of animal mistreatment, cruelty or neglect to the authorities. It is recognised that this may bring negative, as well as positive, benefits – as it may deter some people from seeking medical assistance for their injured animal. However, on balance, such a provision is thought to be favourable.

The authorities are not always in a position to easily discover breaches of the law, and so additional intelligence can be helpful. The aim is not so much reprisal, as assistance for the animal which suffers as well as expert support, advice and help for the keeper by the Competent Authority.

Section 33 (3): The Competent Authority will need to carry out education and awareness activities to encourage citizens to note and report any animal welfare infringements. Providing media feedback on investigations into such complaints will assist to spread the message that public participation is useful and constructive.

Section 33 (4) and (5): The Competent Authority has the duty to follow up on all alerts and reports, and is obligated to file a criminal complaint when a violation according to Section 43 (1) has been committed intentionally.

Section 34 Charges and Fees

The enforcement of the subject Act would in general be free of charge. However, the Minister, the Ministry or the Competent Authority should be entitled to make provisions for the collection of fees or charges in connection with any appropriate and indicated administrative procedures under the Act and subordinate regulations – for example to cover the costs of certain administrative measures such as: authorisations, licenses, permits, certificates, registrations etc., supervision, control and special services. These dues could help with the expenses involved in the execution of this law. It is good practice to collect such dues in a dedicated account, to ensure that they are used for the animal welfare purposes for which they are collected (as opposed to being placed into general government coffers). No costs or charges should be levied in respect of non-profit organisations, or individuals who are carrying out voluntary activities which are deemed to be in the public interest.

Section 35 Animal Welfare Committee

As already mentioned above in IV. Proposed New Measures for Consideration, Involved Parties, an expert Animal Welfare (and Ethics) Committee is needed for a number of purposes. In addition to providing support and counsel to the authorities on a regular basis, these include assisting the government to compile legislation (and enforcement guidance) and to continuously monitor, review and evaluate the existing status and state of animal welfare issues. Expert advice to the government/authorities would include aspects such as: animal care and protection, ethical problems, scientific and legal developments, and practical enforcement issues. Thus, the committee would be charged with keeping abreast of all animal welfare advances, and making recommendations for any policy and enforcement changes needed to take account of these. The Committee would also have a specific duty to ensure that the various agencies in charge of implementing and executing animal welfare laws and provisions are able to effectively carry out their remit.

Section 35 (1): This will include, but not be restricted to, the Animal Welfare Committee compiling a list of traps and catching devices which are authorised, as well as defining which poisons are allowable in which circumstances (positive lists).

Section 35 (2): It is important that members of the Committee are appointed on a personal basis, so they can always put animal welfare interests first, regardless of their official position or role. In an Animal Welfare Committee, the primary duty should always be to the welfare of animals. Thus, members should be selected based on their personal expertise, experience and sympathy to animal welfare. Ethical training is considered necessary to ensure that each member is able to weigh the different ethical perspectives – which can be complex in animal welfare. Issue-related Sub-Committees have been included here in order to ensure appropriate expertise and consideration: This avoids the situation where every Committee member has to be involved in the minutiae of every issue.

Section 35 (3): The Committee must be granted free and full access to all government information and statistics (and premises for the purpose of cross-checking), and at the same time it has to be ensured that it is in a position to publish critical and/or controversial reports or statements when required (including minority reports). An annual report is not only a record of its work during the year, but also a permanent record of its recommendations to government and the status of governments' response to these (including any that have not yet been actioned). There must always be openness and transparency in its work.

Section 36   Animal Welfare Ombudsman

This provision for the appointment of an Animal Welfare Ombudsman provides both an independent arbiter for animal welfare issues, and enhanced legal protection for animals. [NB. 'Ombudsman' is a known concept and term, and is used in this Act to cover both male and female incumbents of the post.] The provision of legal representation for animals has been added in order to ensure that animals can (where required) be provided with the necessary and appropriate protection under the law (which they are not able to assess and request on their own account). Thus a 'public protector' now is tasked with maintaining/defending the interests of the individual animal. Some countries already use Animal Welfare Ombudsmen and the system is now being called for in others (including Australia and the EU). Switzerland used to have an animal lawyer to act on behalf of the interests of the individual animal in criminal proceedings concerning offences against animal welfare legislation but unfortunately abolished this function by the end of 2010. However, it is considered of utmost importance to provide representation of an individual animal's own interests at both administrative and criminal levels. The main advantage of this representation over the use of the Public Prosecutor is the level of knowledge/expertise, and the fact that this would be a priority function for the Animal Welfare Ombudsman's office.

Section 36 (2): Relevant professional qualifications may vary and need to be balanced with skills and experience. These must in combination be sufficient to provide a solid technical and practical overview of animal welfare science, ethics and practical issues. Relevant professional studies may include (but not be limited to): veterinary medicine, animal behaviour/ethology and animal welfare law.

Section 37   Animal Welfare and Protection
Organisations/Humane Societies

Section 37 (1): This provision should guarantee that always all parties and stakeholders with a verifiable interest in animal welfare and protection issues shall have a chance to be heard and be given an opportunity to influence any current or future measures which might be considered by the authorities/government.

Section 37 (2): This provision guards against commercial interests using the designation 'animal welfare organisation', 'animal protection organisation' or 'humane society' in order to collect funds and donations for purposes other than animal welfare.

Section 37 (3) - (5): Some countries where resources for animal welfare enforcement are scarce (man-power and finances) may decide to supplement official enforcement by engaging animal welfare and protection organisations/humane societies in the enforcement task (or in selected parts of this). If this approach is adopted, it is preferable to limit engagement to organisations/societies which have been previously approved by the Minister/Ministry or Competent Authority and fulfil certain requirements according to sub-section (4).

There will need to be discussion and consultation to decide the extent to which enforcement powers should, could or would be given to animal welfare and protection organisations/humane societies. This will relate to both the level of powers ceded by the Competent Authority and the extent to which animal welfare and protection organisations/humane societies are willing to assume government tasks (and whether such services should be compensated).

For their part, animal welfare and protection organisations/humane societies will need to give careful consideration to whether they consider enforcement and prosecution as part of their mission, or whether their willingness to accept such a role could facilitate the 'abdication' of government for their responsibilities in this area and/or whether the work would detract from their other programmes (such as government monitoring, advocacy, and education and awareness).

Animal welfare and protection organisations/humane societies will also need to give careful consideration to the effectiveness and viability of accepting enforcement responsibilities, including the extent to which they are given the powers and resources required for the successful discharge of enforcement duties. Here the matter of costs and resources is also an important issue: Animal welfare and protection organisations/humane societies always need to secure funds for their work. Thus, they should negotiate satisfactory government reimbursement for any expenses incurred in carrying out such delegated enforcement measures.

In addition to giving the Animal Welfare Ombudsman the authority of legal representation of an individual animal one might also contemplate allowing any approved Animal Welfare and Protection Organisation/Humane Society the right of action within the framework of an altruistic legal action, i.e. to file complaints against sovereign decisions without being prejudiced in its own rights. Whereby here once again the public interest would be paramount as this right of action for Animal Welfare and Protection Organisations/Humane Societies would only cover infringements of any objectives rights to the detriment of animals but would not apply to an assertion of any possible subjective rights of an individual animal.

Section 38   Animal Shelters, Animal Sanctuaries and Wildlife Rehabilitation Centres

Running an animal shelter, animal sanctuary or wildlife rehabilitation centre also requires authorisation in accordance with Section 29. This will prevent the establishment of inadequate facilities and/or facilities being established by ill-qualified and/or unsuitable individuals.

Section 38 (1): As well-run animal shelters, animal sanctuaries and wildlife rehabilitation centres can be beneficial for wildlife and society, it was decided not to restrict these activities to registered non-profit organisations. However, it was decided appropriate to restrict donations (please see Section 38 (6)) to registered non-profit organisations (as these can be accounted for and controlled, to ensure they are used for the purpose).

Section 38 (4): There are a number of measures taken by shelters worldwide to ensure that animals adopted before spay-neuter is possible are subsequently spay-neutered. One option requires adopting owners to leave a financial deposit with the shelter, which is refunded when the dog or cat is brought in for the scheduled operation at the appropriate age/fitness. Alternatively, ownership registration requirements could also be used here: allowing animals to be temporarily homed without official transfer of ownership until they are returned for the operation.
The procedures used by shelters for spay-neuter returns could form part of the competent authority's authorisation checks.

Section 38 (5): It is important to restrict use of these names (animal shelter, animal sanctuary or wildlife rehabilitation centre) to bona fide organisations to prevent the (current) proliferation of these terms simply to secure visitors and support fraudulently.

A system of licensing has been suggested for animal shelters, sanctuaries and wildlife rehabilitation centres. However, it is possible to amend this to another form of authorisation (e.g. registration or certification), if appropriate to the system of the jurisdiction.

Section 38 (7): Such additional provisions could include

- Providing definitions for an 'animal shelter', 'animal sanctuary' and 'wildlife rehabilitation centre' – which have to be met in order to qualify under each distinct category;
- Establishing detailed standards and criteria which must be met in order to be licensed as an authorised animal shelter, animal sanctuary or wildlife rehabilitation centre; or
- Establishing Welfare Codes containing 'best practice' for each category.

In delineating secondary legislation and guidelines, the Competent Authority will need to place particular attention on the following: that the animal taken into the custody of an animal shelter, animal sanctuary or wildlife rehabilitation centre receives all the attention needed, including ample medical care, as well as appropriate housing and surroundings adapted to its species-specific requirements. Detailed provisions covering the important record keeping requirements (see Section 38 (4)) will have to be established, including: animals arriving and departing from the facility. In addition, rules will need to be elaborated covering the management of the animal, including: the knowledge, experience, expertise and technical skills of the person who will run the animal shelter, animal sanctuary or wildlife rehabilitation centre.

'Animal shelter', 'animal sanctuary' and 'wildlife rehabilitation centre' have each been defined within the Act (see Section 5 Pt. 3., Pt. 2. and Pt. 28.), and are distinctly different. Thus it is important that each license is issued accordingly (with relevant criteria and conditions). A brief overview of the key differences is

Animal Shelter: Temporarily houses and cares for stray or homeless animals, in order to reunite them with their owners or rehome them;

Animal Santuary: Keeps animals to live out their lives; and

Wildlife Rehabilitation Centre: Cares for injured, orphaned, or sick wild animals with the aim of returning them to the wild after treatment and rehabilitation.

When drafting conditions for the licensing of sanctuaries, it is important to ensure that these provide for optimum conditions, as close as possible to the relevant species' native habitat, as the animals will be there for life. Wildlife rehabilitation centres should have a similar provision, as they are for wild animals that need to remain accustomed to conditions in the wild: In order to be successfully rehabilitated, it is important that they stay in near-natural conditions without becoming accustomed to human contact or proximity.

Section 39   Veterinarians and Para-Veterinarians

As animal health and welfare professionals, veterinarians and para-veterinarians are on the front-line of caring for animals thus they should always prioritise the animal's health and well-being and not focus primarily on their duty to the animal's owner. However, many are paid for their services by the industry, which may lead to a conflict of interest which has the potential to jeopardise the health and welfare of animals. These provisions have been included to counter this possibility.

Section 39 (3): This clause requiring veterinarians and para-veterinarians to report (potential) cases of non-compliance with this Act has been added after careful consideration. It is recognised that one possible adverse effect of this provision may be that owners or keepers are unwilling to bring suffering animals for veterinary attention. However, it strengthens their duty of care, and core role as protectors of the health and welfare of animals – which is viewed as widely beneficial.

Section 40   Animal Welfare Research

National animal welfare research is necessary in addition to available international research to ensure that the country can take decisions and share knowledge and expertise about animal welfare issues, on the basis of evidence which is relevant to local conditions and the local situation.

Section 41   Consumer Information

These provisions are designed to ensure that consumers are provided with adequate information on the animal welfare aspects of products, thereby empowering them to make informed choices and drive further improvements in animal welfare.

In cases where countries decide not to ban any system or method which is known to cause, or likely to cause, animal welfare problems, then the Competent Authority shall specifically require products made using this system or method to be clearly labelled as such. This will include, but not be limited to, meat produced from animals in (or born from parents in) close confinement systems (cages, stalls, crates etc.) and products tested on animals.

Section 42   Animal Welfare Measurement and Impact Assessment

This Section provides for Animal Welfare Impact Assessments to be carried out routinely whenever animal welfare could be adversely impacted. This practice is already widely carried out in relation to environmental issues (as an environmental impact assessment). This is particularly useful for determining any potential impact on wildlife populations of any planned development activities or change of land use. But it could also be useful in other areas – for example, impact on animals in rural areas – such as: development or building activities, deforestation, changing water courses (dams, flooding, river works etc.), changes to habitat etc. It would also cover aspects not usually connected to animal issues, such as the use of chemicals, herbicides, pesticides etc.

Section 42 (2): When animal welfare legislation has been agreed, it is important to ensure that other government policies and laws do not undermine or contradict this. Thus the need for an audit of these; and amendments made whenever necessary to adhere to animal welfare principles.

Section 42 (4): Animal welfare indicators should comprise all authorised/licensed uses. These will need to cover all species, and both inputs (i.e. needs to be provided for the animal, including stockmanship) and animal based measures (ABMs). Inputs are needed to ensure that welfare can be provided for, but only the condition of the animals can procure a true indication of the state of the animal (and thus its welfare). These indicators need to include clear, measurable requirements which allow animal keepers and official Animal Welfare Inspectors to assess compliance. Once agreed, the indicators will need to be publicised and animal owners, keepers and users educated.

Section 42 (5): Statistics are needed to identify and analyse any problems with particular animal industries and uses. This enables the Competent Authority to plan future interventions (such as education/training, enforcement targeting and legislative amendment).

CHAPTER 6: PENAL AND FINAL/CONCLUDING PROVISIONS

Section 43   Penal and Administrative Fine Provisions

Penalties should be set by the Competent Authority according to a fine banding system which would be preferable to actually stating any specific amount in any currency in the subject Act itself. The actual currency levels for each banding shall then be stipulated in regulations or published in the Official Gazette (calculated by taking into account the severity of the infringement, and average income and general living standards of each individual country). Then these can be reviewed on a regular basis, and easily amended when required, according to inflation rates.

By way of example, the list of fine levels for each banding could be established as follows:

Level 1 offence – minor infringements – penalties set at a minimum of Euro 50 up to Euro 1,000;
Level 2 offence – serious infringements – penalties set at a minimum of Euro 300 up to Euro 15,000, and for corporate bodies up to Euro 50,000;
Level 3 offence – aggravated infringements as well as repeated offences – penalties set at a minimum of Euro 3,000 up to Euro 30,000, and for corporate bodies up to Euro 250,000; and
Level 4 offence – for criminal offences imprisonment of up to 5 years and a fine of minimum Euro 5,000 up to Euro 250,000, and for corporate bodies up to Euro 500,000.

Please note that these amounts are only a guide, and appropriate levels would need to be determined for each country. Also, please note that this currency guidance has been determined at the date of publication of this Model Animal Welfare Act and may become outdated over time (the very reason we promote a banding system). In no case should lower penalties be established than those existing for any law that the Act supersedes. Thus any country using this Act as a basis for a new Animal Welfare Act is advised to read each section carefully, and to compare with any existing provisions to ensure that this is providing an enhancement and improvement to the exiting level of protection and deterrent.

In some countries, fines are related not only to the seriousness of the offence, but also to the economic situation of the offender. This can be a just system, if well applied – in particular to ensure that fines are established at meaningful levels for more affluent individuals. The same rationale is applied to the provision of higher maximum fine levels for corporate bodies.

Fines for animal mistreatment have to be substantial enough to function not only as adequate punishment, but also as a suitable and effective deterrent.

However, deterrence and punishment – as well as education and further training – should always go hand in hand: And the hope is that these will eventually achieve a shift in human attitudes and behaviour.

Section 44 Prohibition of Keeping Animals or of Having Contact with Animals and Forfeiture

This is an important provision – for both its deterrent value and its role in preventing further animal welfare problems.

Section 45 Further Aspects

The list of further aspects is not comprehensive, but should highlight a few points worthy of further consideration.

The financial implications to be addressed would also depend very much on the individual country and the scale of expenditure. For instance, as regards creating or updating an existing or new administrative apparatus to combine and supervise all animal welfare related activities.

Some auxiliary costs could be compensated by charging fees for certain administrative measures, i.e. for authorisations, licenses, permits, supervision, control as well as specific services under the subject Act and subordinate regulations stipulated under the Act according to Section 34 (2).